Philosophy of Revolution

Towards a Non-Leninist Marxism

Lenny Flank

Red and Black Publishers, St Petersburg, Florida 2007

Publishers Cataloging in Publication Data –

Flank, Lenny, 1961-

　Philosophy of Revolution: Towards a Non-Leninist Marxism/Lenny Flank

　p. cm.

　Includes bibliographical references.

　ISBN: 978-0-9791813-8-2

1. Communism

I. Title

HX.237 F53 2007

335.009　　　　　LCCN: 2007932147

Red and Black Publishers, PO Box 7542, St Petersburg, Florida, 33734

Contact us at: info@RedandBlackPublishers.com

Printed and manufactured in the United States of America

CONTENTS

Introduction

After the success of the 1917 Revolution in Russia and the rise of the Third International, the Leninist model of socialism and revolution enjoyed widespread acceptance. Nearly every revolution, rebellion or revolt that has occurred over the past hundred years has been Leninist in inspiration and in structure.

The recent collapse of these countries, however, has made clear the weaknesses and deficiencies in Leninist theory and practice. The death of the Leninist nations and their overthrow by popular rebellions were visible examples of the bankruptcy of the Leninist organizational and political model.

In the period between the World Wars, however, an entirely different trend of socialist thought had briefly flowered in Europe and the United States, a trend which rejected the Leninist model of revolutionary organization and which affirmed the complete self-emancipation of the working class from capitalist domination. This movement was "council communism" — the idea that the workers themselves should control their destiny, free from the domination of any boss or any political faction. In Europe, this movement was inspired and led by the writings of Pannekoek, Gorter, Korsch, and

Gramsci. In the United States, the council movement was represented by the syndicalist Industrial Workers of the World (IWW), or "Wobblies". In the 60's and 70's, council ideas took the form of militant direct actions, particularly as put forth by the "urban guerrilla" school of Renate Curcio, Carlos Marighella and Abraham Guillen.

With the rise of Leninist and Stalinist regimes in Russia and elsewhere, the Leninist conception took on the air of Holy Writ, and the dissenting council communist movement was hounded, harassed and eventually broken.

Today, however, as the fundamentals of Leninism are discredited and rejected, the theory and practice of the council communists have increasing relevance. Syndicalist and worker council theories played a large role in the Hungarian workers' revolution of 1956, in the armed struggles which took place in Italy in the 1970's, and in the revolts in Eastern Europe in 1989 (spearheaded by the Polish Solidarity labor union) which swept away the Leninist dictatorships. As the major capitalist nations continue to face yet another period of economic slowdown and crisis, the theory and practice of council communism will grow in importance and relevance.

The purpose of this book is, therefore, to present a synopsis of the goals and actions of the non-Leninist council communist movement. And since, in my opinion, the council movement is the most complete expression of the outlooks and insights of Marxian philosophy, it also serves as a synopsis of the thoughts and actions of Karl Marx. Despite its mistakes and inaccuracies, the Marxian framework is important in understanding the functioning of the capitalist system.

Those who are looking for mere intellectual abstraction and theory, however, will not find it here. The council communist movement is above all a practical movement, and finds its purpose in direct working class action. Like Marx, we disdain to conceal our views, and we openly declare that our goal is that of revolution, of the overthrow of the capitalist system and its substitution by worker-managed socialism. Between "philosophy" and "revolution", the council movement emphasizes the need for both.

ONE:
Fundamentals of Marxian Philosophy

In his philosophical inquiry, Marx set out to answer essentially the same questions asked by Hegel; "What is the nature of human social reality?" and "What is the source of human social reality?"

From the earliest days of human history, people have attempted to explain the source of reality by referring to a force or being which stood "outside of reality" and directed it according to some "supernatural plan". Thus, ancient peoples presented the notion that reality is controlled by "the gods", and that the actions of the gods could be interpreted and explained through the medium of religion.

The idea that supernatural forces and religious thought were the directors of reality was strong in Marx's time (and still is today), and Marx devoted a considerable amount of effort to refute this notion. "Criticism of religion", wrote Marx, "is in the main complete, and the criticism of religion is the premise of all criticism."

In his criticism of religion, Marx leans heavily on the concept of "alienation". All religious thought, Marx points out, was made and produced by humans: humans wrote the major religious texts, humans devised the various myths and legends which describe the gods, humans perform the tasks of interpreting these religious beliefs. Thus, all religious thought is the product of human thought—humans are not made in the image of God; rather, god has been made by humans in the image of humans. "The basis of irreligious criticism," Marx writes, "is, man makes religion; religion does not make man. Religion is the self-consciousness and self-esteem of man who has either not yet found himself or has already lost himself again."

Religious thought, however, is unable to conceive of itself as being merely distorted human thought which has been transported to an "other-worldly" or "supernatural" plane. Religion, despite the fact that it was itself created by human thoughts and actions, continues to view itself as a separate and distinct entity with no connection to human thought, will or agency. Although religious thought is a human-made creation, it is treated as though it were capable of creating humans and controlling their actions. Similarly, a human who carves a wooden idol may give that idol supernatural powers and fall down and worship it, never realizing that the object of his religious fervor was created by human hands and has no power in itself.

Marx thus concluded that religious thought was merely human thought which has been separated or "alienated" from the human reality which created it; it was merely human thought which has been given the appearance of an independent existence. As such, it cannot be the source of reality, since it itself is not real, and has its origin in the human thoughts from which it has become alienated. "The task of history, therefore," Marx concludes, "once the world beyond the truth has disappeared, is to establish the truth of this world. The immediate task of philosophy, which is at the service of history, is to unmask self-estrangement in its unholy forms."

Up to this point, Marx has not left the framework established by Hegel. Hegel, too, viewed religious thought as an illusory abstraction from human thought. Hegel's criticism of religion led him to the realm of philosophy known as idealism. If religion is simply alienated human thought, Hegel concluded, then the source of social reality must lie in the human ideas from which religious thought is abstracted. Hegelian dialectical idealism is based on the conclusion that the source of human social organization lies in the ideas of that social group of humans.

It did not take Marx long to reject this notion. The complicated and high-sounding philosophical treatises of the Hegelians, Marx concluded, themselves have no connection to reality; they exist only in the intellectual sphere. Like the religious thought which was criticized by Hegel, the philosophers had transformed their thought into an independent realm, free of connections to the real world. "Hitherto," Marx wrote, "men have constantly made up for themselves false conceptions about themselves, about what they are and what they ought to be . . . The phantoms of their brains have gotten out of their hands:"

> For philosophers, one of the most difficult tasks is to descend from the world of thought to the actual world. Language is the immediate actuality of thought. Just as philosophers have given thought an independent existence, so they had to make language into an independent realm. This is the secret of philosophical language, in which thoughts in the form of words have their own content. The problems of descending from the world of thoughts to the actual world is turned into the problem of descending from language to life. . . The philosophers would only have to dissolve their language into the ordinary language, from which it is abstracted, to recognize it as the distorted language of the actual world, and to realize that neither thoughts nor language in themselves form a realm of their own, that they are only manifestations of actual life.

Ideas and philosophy, Marx concluded, cannot be the source of reality, because these ideas are themselves abstracted from human existence and experiences. Philosophical language and thoughts are merely the idealized expressions of actual human experiences within an existing social reality. In claiming that these ideas are the moving force behind social reality, the philosophers fail to mention that these ideas must first themselves be produced, and that the philosophers who attempt to educate us to them must first themselves be educated; that is, they must receive their ideas from some source.

Since philosophers live within existing social reality, Marx postulated, the source of their ideas and philosophy must also lie in their social surroundings. If human ideas are to be fully understood, the material realities and social circumstances which produce them must be understood as well. As Marx puts it:

> One has to "leave philosophy aside", one has to leap out of it and devote oneself like an ordinary man to the study of actuality. . . Philosophy and the study of the actual world have the same relationship to one another as masturbation and sexual intercourse.

Marx's rejection of Hegelian idealism led him to begin the study of the materialist school of philosophy, which holds that reality is the product of a mechanistic chain of cause and effect. In effect, the materialists assert, the universe is a giant machine which runs according to eternal and unalterable "natural laws". Humans are powerless to avoid these laws, and the universe operates independently of the actions or will of humans.

In particular, Marx studied the writings of Ludwig Feuerbach, himself a student of Hegel who had rejected Hegelian idealism. Marx found himself quickly disappointed. While idealism tended to emphasize the action of human ideas on the structure of social reality, materialism tends to reduce humanity to a cog in an impersonal machine, in a deterministic social situation about which humans can do little.

Marx strongly rejected this argument. Materialism, he wrote, mistakenly emphasizes the material side of reality without taking note of the non-material:

> The chief defect of all materialism up to now (including Feuerbach's) is that the object, reality, which we apprehend through our senses, is understood only in the form of the subject of contemplation; but not as sensuous human activity, as practice; not subjectively. Hence in opposition to materialism the active side was developed abstractly by idealism—which does not know real sensuous activity as such.

Feuerbach's notion of blind, deterministic materialism failed to account for the human capacity for voluntarism, for our ability to change our material surroundings through willful actions. Since human ideas are capable of influencing our surroundings, the source of social reality cannot be wholly material. However, since these ideas are themselves abstractions from existing circumstances, the source of social reality cannot be wholly ideal either.

Marx found the answer to this puzzle in a combination of materialism and idealism into the system now known as philosophical naturalism. Naturalism as a philosophy holds that human social reality is partly a product of existing circumstances and partly a product of willful actions upon those circumstances—one part nature and one part nurture.

The human sides of physicality and spirituality are united in reality precisely in the fact that they are human—that is, both matter and idea are united within human existence. Human social reality can thus be seen to be the product of human social reality. The criticism of religion and philosophy therefore leads to the conclusion that humanity is the ultimate source of humanity, and that human reality can only be grasped through a humanist framework. "To be radical," wrote Marx, "is to grasp things by the root. But for man, the root is man himself."

Marx was thus led into a study of existing human circumstances and of the uniqueness of humanity's interactions with its surroundings. All other natural beings, i.e., plants and animals, are born with the devices and instincts which they need to survive. Only humans are born with no weapons, no means of keeping warm, no method of producing food. Humans are thus out of necessity moved to create tools, constructions, etc., in order to carry on their physical existence, and these various items are fashioned from materials found in nature. Thus, humans must maintain a constant interaction with their natural surroundings if they are to survive. Marx writes, "Nature is man's inorganic body—nature, that is, insofar as it is not itself human body. Man lives in nature—means that nature is his body, with which he must remain in continuous intercourse if he is not to die."

At the same time, Marx realized, by using human labor power to modify natural materials and provide the means of life, humanity is constantly changing nature—existing circumstances and surroundings are constantly being altered by human actions. These changes in existing circumstances, in turn, make it necessary to modify human actions in order to enforce the requirements of this new set of circumstances. Human ideas and actions change human surroundings, and are themselves altered by these changes. Humanity thus creates its surroundings at the same time as those surroundings create humanity.

This constant and simultaneous interplay is the dialectic. A dialectical relationship is one in which the actors are interdependent, with each determined by and also determining the other. Human thoughts and action can be seen to be a unity, an interpenetrating relationship which, though in conflict, is nevertheless united in humanity's relationship with nature.

To study the nature of this relationship, however, it is necessary to study real, actual human beings. Marx writes, "The first premise of human history is, of course, the existence of living human individuals. Thus the first fact to be established is the organization of these individuals and their consequent relationship to the rest of nature."

The most basic requirement for a group of humans is to survive and procreate—to obtain food, shelter, clothing, etc., and to reproduce the species. In all of these tasks, constant interaction between human individuals is necessary. In other words, humans must form a social network in order to maintain their existence. Thus, human reality is above all a social reality, and human actions are above all social actions.

In order to live by the process of modifying natural products, humans must construct a social framework which allows them to use their labor power for this purpose. In other words, they must construct a definite set of social relationships which enable them to produce the necessaries of life and to distribute these to the members of the social group. Marx called this social structure a "mode of production", which becomes for these humans the social reality from which their ideas are abstracted. As Marx puts it:

> This mode of production must not be considered simply as being the reproduction of the physical existence of these individuals. Rather, it is a definite form of activity of these individuals, a definite mode of life on their part.

Since human actions and natural surroundings are constantly modifying each other, it can be readily seen that this system of human organization is not a static one. Social reality, far from being a cold and lifeless entity, is a dynamic and restless process of development and change. Social reality and all of its interrelationships are in a constant state of both being what they are and of becoming something else. This conclusion is central to the Marxian conception of human history. Marx writes:

> The materialist conception of history starts from the proposition that the production of the means to support human life and, alongside production, the exchange of things produced is the basis of all social structure; that in every society that has appeared in history, the manner in which wealth is distributed and society divided into classes

or orders is dependent upon what is produced, how it is produced, and how the products are exchanged.

It is important to remember that, while human thought and actions can produce changes in social reality, they cannot do so under conditions or circumstances dictated by humans. The human who is born in a particular time and place must deal with social and natural reality as it exists, not as humans would like it to be. Any given human society can only operate within the circumstances which it finds bequeathed to it—it must use the technology, knowledge and material reality which have been passed on to it by its predecessors. What *is* is inescapably the product of what *was*.

In this process of change which social reality undergoes, human social relationships must be constantly modified to conform to these new circumstances. These social relationships, in turn, are based on the necessity of producing the means of life from natural surroundings. Each specific relationship between human society and its natural surroundings will produce the social framework which is best suited for allowing humans to live within those surroundings. Human thought and actions can modify this social framework, but these changes must always stay within the limits imposed by the need to extract the necessities of life from existing circumstances.

Human social actions are thus placed under severe restraints by specific historical and material circumstances. People cannot move their social organization in any random direction they desire; they can only move within the framework allowed to them by existing circumstances.

In the dialectical process of social development, then, changes in material surroundings which are brought about by social actions produce the need for new methods of social organization. When these changes have reached a certain point, the existing system of social relationships is no longer suited for dealing with existing circumstances, and it must be replaced by a new form of social organization, a new "mode of production". Human history can thus be viewed as the process whereby one social mode of production replaces another, in response to changes in material reality brought about through human social practice.

Within each mode of production, moreover, human society is organized around definite social relationships which serve to embody, protect, maintain and procreate that system of social organization. These social relationships are built around the need to produce and distribute the means of life, and, since this is the focus of the science of economics, it may be said that the motivation behind human social action is economic in nature. As Marx puts it, "From this point of view the final cause of all social changes and revolutions are to be sought, not in men's brains, not in men's better insights into eternal truth and justice, but in changes in the mode of production and exchange. They are to be sought not in the philosophy but in the economics of each particular epoch."

As these social structures change, so too must the political, economic, religious and philosophical ideas which permeate them and support them (and which are after all merely idealized abstractions from existing circumstances).

This does not mean, as many Leninists have mistakenly assumed, that Marx was an "economic determinist", who believed that material economic changes are the sole sources of social change. Marx recognized that the social and material realm can be influenced and changed (sometimes drastically) by human thoughts and willful actions. Nevertheless, it remains true that these actions can only influence the mode of production within the limits imposed by the necessity of working within existing circumstances. Marx summarizes his view of social development:

> The fact is, therefore, that definite individuals who are productively active in a definite way enter into these definite social and political relations. Empirical observation must in each separate instance bring out empirically, and without any mystification and speculation, the connection of the social and political structure with production. The social structure and the state are continually evolving out of the

life-processes of definite individuals, but of individuals not as they appear in their own or in other people's imaginations, but as they really are, i.e.. as they operate, produce materially and hence as they work under definite material limits, presuppositions and conditions independent of their will.

Thus convinced of the importance of economic factors in the development of human history, Marx began a period of intense study of classical economics, including Ricardo, Say and Smith. In his study of economic structures, Marx recognized that, within each mode of production, relationships appear between groups of people who perform similar economic and social tasks and who thus interrelate in a similar socio-economic manner. Marx referred to these socio-politico-economic groupings as "classes", and they took on a crucial importance in the Marxian conception of history. While all of the social classes are in social unity with each other — that is, each is necessary for the functioning of the mode of production — the motives and interests of these classes are implacably opposed, and a constant struggle rages between them.

The ruling class, the one that has the most control over the means of production and obtains the most benefit from it, uses social relationships to maintain this position of privilege. Thus, while society's economic, legal, philosophical and ethical systems are formed from the necessity to form and propagate the mode of production, these spheres are also utilized by the ruling class to safeguard its privileged position within this mode of production. Class struggle in the political, economic and ideological spheres rages constantly, as the oppressed and exploited classes attempt to overthrow the ruling class and change the social structure in their favor. "The history of all hitherto society," Marx wrote, "is the history of class struggles."

Of course, this class struggle can, for the most part, only influence the development of the social mode of production within the definite limits imposed by the need to interact with existing reality. When the material conditions have changed to the point where a new social mode becomes necessary, however, a class or classes of the old mode of production will find that it can introduce a new mode that fits both its own subjective interests and the objective necessities of existing circumstances.

The ruling class which benefits from the old mode will attempt to prevent this for as long as possible, using its control of the economic, political and ideological spheres to coerce and repress the rising new class, but in the end the old order of things is doomed. It is no longer able to relate to its surroundings effectively, and is no longer able to provide and distribute the necessaries of life to the members of human society. When this happens, the old ruling class is destroyed by the rising class, in a social, political and economic upheaval that shatters the old social order and builds a new mode of production on its ruins. A new world rises from the ashes of the old.

In the capitalist mode of production, society is increasingly divided into two hostile classes: the bourgeoisie, who own capital and who therefore hold the position of privilege in this social order, and the proletariat, who own no capital and who live only by selling their labor power to the capitalists. The bourgeoisie, by virtue of its control over the means of production, also claims the dominant position in the social relationships of law, ethics, morality and ideology, and uses these to safeguard its position of privilege and dominance.

Although the class struggle between the bourgeoisie and proletariat rages in all social spheres, the most directly visible arena is the economic. The capitalist mode of production, in contrast to feudal and other modes, uses economic relationships directly to justify and continue the bourgeoisie's control of the social order. While the feudal aristocrats used religious terminology and authority to justify their privileged position, the capitalists use an alienated economic ideology to maintain their position. Capitalist economic structures and relationships are made to appear as an independent and eternal part of reality, made up of impersonal "laws" — the "rule of the marketplace". Human members of society, according to this outlook, are rewarded or punished by this "invisible hand," which controls the actions of humanity with the irresistible force of natural law.

In reality, we can see that these "natural economic laws" are merely abstracted and idealized forms of the human relationships which exist under the capitalist mode of production. Marx illustrates this point with the example of the "fetishism of commodities". According to the precepts of capitalist economics, the exchange of commodities is "regulated" through the mechanism of the marketplace, which compels people to act in certain ways. Thus, the commodity marketplace is viewed as an impersonal "thing", a separately existing entity which has the power to control the actions of humans. The commodity marketplace, however, as Marx points out, has no existence of its own apart from the social relationships which produced it. Marketplaces can do nothing "on their own", and are incapable of "regulating" anything or "performing any actions"; they are merely abstractions of the concrete relationships between those who own capital and those who do not. If the social relationships between workers and owners would be broken, the marketplace would no longer exist as a marketplace—indeed, capitalism would no longer exist as capitalism. For the capitalists to create a market economy and then give that market the power to regulate human actions makes no more sense than for a person to carve an idol and then allow that idol to determine human actions.

Study of the capitalist economy, therefore, led Marx right back to what he considered to be the starting point of any study of human history—to a study of the existing social relationships which constitute any given mode of production. For the rest of his life, Marx devoted himself to a study of the relationships which make up the bourgeois mode of production, and to a study of the dialectical interactions which alter these relationships and which will ultimately produce the downfall of the capitalist system and its substitution by socialism.

TWO:
Fundamentals of Marxian Economics

The basis of Marxian economics is fundamentally different from that of bourgeois capitalist economics. Capitalist economics takes the form of "objectively" examining the "laws" of the capitalist marketplace, of determining the workings of these "impartial laws" and to apply these lessons to economic activities.

Marxists, on the other hand, recognize that all of these economic "laws" are merely alienated abstractions from social reality — merely the idealized versions of existing social relationships.

The Marxist, therefore, studies the economy from the point of view of the social relationships which make it up. Rather than asserting that human actions are the products of impartial economic "laws", Marxists conclude that these economic structures are themselves the products of human thought and actions, which are in turn responses to the specific circumstances within which these human beings find themselves. Marxian economics, then, is the study of these underlying social relationships.

Marxian economics, then, does not accept many of the implicit assumptions made by capitalist economists. Capitalism, as the capitalists themselves tell us, is based primarily upon the notion of "private property", which, according to bourgeois ideology, is an unchanging part of the human condition, one of the "inalienable rights of man".

In fact, as the Marxist economist points out, private property is a social relationship, and has its basis in the fact that the means of production in the capitalist system are owned by one small segment of the population and not by the rest. Thus, although the institution of private ownership of capital appears in bourgeois society as an impersonal power that controls the relationship between worker and owner, in fact it is the idealized expression of the capitalist's dominant social position over the workers.

The same can be seen to be true about the work process which is so much a part of the capitalist system. The worker labors in a factory, where each is assigned to a particular task to insure the greatest possible profitability. The pyramidal organization of the factory, in the capitalist schema, is presented as an inescapable necessity, as an unchangeable notion of "how things get done". In fact, it is another consequence of the relationship between labor and capital. In capitalist ideology, humans must serve the needs of industry and production, rather than placing the process of industrial production at the service of humanity. Since the capitalist owns and benefits from industrial production, this safeguards the capitalist's position of privilege. The factory system is but an expression of the bourgeoisie's dominant position as ruling class. It is a social relationship, not an eternal economic "given".

The error of all the bourgeois economists, as Marx sees it, lies precisely in the fact that they take the alienated capitalist ideology as reality—they view economics as the motion of independent categories and "things": Labor, Capital, Commodity, the Marketplace. All of these are the results of relationships between humans, however, and none has any real power over humans. Thus, while the bourgeois capitalists view workers as personified Labor and owners as personified Capital, the Marxist treats this as an alienation, and asserts that Labor is nothing more than idealized workers, Capital is nothing other than abstracted owners, and the Marketplace is simply the alienated conception of the relationship between the members of a capitalist society.

In the earlier modes of production, economic activity served the simple purpose of producing the various items which were necessary for the maintenance of life—food, clothing, shelter, tools, etc. The primary purpose of producing these items was their utility, or, as Marx puts it, their "use-value". In these modes of production, the position of the ruling class was maintained less by economic means than by the use of religious and ethical notions. The feudal doctrines of Divine Right and chivalry, for instance, insured that a large portion of the things which were produced went to the ruling class, which did little or nothing to produce them.

In the capitalist mode of production, however, economic relationships serve directly to appropriate a portion of the social product and to justify and defend this appropriation. This process revolves around the "commodity". In the Marxian conception, a commodity is a product which is produced for the purpose of exchange or sale rather than for its utility to the producer—for its exchange-value, not its use-value.

Under the earliest commodity exchange system, barter, commodities were exchanged directly for each other whenever each producer had a surplus over what could be used. Later, production was begun with exchange specifically in mind, and money was introduced as an intermediary to facilitate this exchange.

Under the earliest simple commodity exchange relationships (which appeared in force during the last half of the feudal period), the economic, relationship is one of:

$$C - M - C$$

where C represents a commodity and M is the monetary medium of exchange. In this economic transaction, the producer makes a certain commodity C and converts it into a sum of money corresponding to its exchange-value. This monetary equivalent is then exchanged for the new desired commodity C.

In this relationship, the values of the exchanged commodities are equal, and no new value is created; the price of the final product is the same as that of the original commodity. Thus, this form of economic relationship cannot serve as the basis for a social order in which one class exploits another by appropriating products from it through economic exchange.

In the capitalist mode of production, however, economic exchange serves precisely this purpose. In the capitalist mode, the role of money is expanded. It is no longer simply a method of facilitating exchange—it now becomes a means of expanding wealth and of appropriating a portion of the social product. It becomes capital.

This economic relationship can only exist when a class within society has obtained a virtual monopoly on wealth in the form of money. Unlike the earlier simple commodity exchange relationship, which was always peripheral to the mode of production, the bourgeoisie's monopoly on capital is absolutely central to the capitalist social system and affects all of its social relationships.

The capitalist economic formula is one of:

$$M - C - M'$$

In this relationship, the capitalist invests a sum M of his capital and uses this to produce a commodity C for exchange. M' (pronounced "M-prime") is the monetary sum the capitalist receives in exchange for the commodities. At the end of the process, the sum M' is greater than the sum M. In other words, through the process of production and exchange, the capitalist is able to expand capital and appropriate a portion of social wealth.

The dominant position of the capitalist in this scheme is thus, contrary to what the bourgeois economists would have us believe, not due to the capitalist's "business sense" or "entrepreneurial skills" or "superior business acumen"; it is due solely to the fact that the capitalist class, and it alone, owns capital.

Because the capitalist class holds the dominant position in these production and exchange relationships, it is able to construct a socio-political system which, while producing the necessary means of life for society, nevertheless also diverts a large portion of these products to the capitalist class.

In the simple non-capitalist form of commodity exchange, it was noted that the values of the bartered commodities were equal, and that neither partner created any new wealth in the exchange. To determine how this is so, it is necessary to introduce some method of measuring the exchange-value of the bartered commodities, so that the trading partners can assure themselves that the exchange is equal. The method developed by the classical economists and adopted by Marx was the theory of labor value.

As we have already noted, humans are the only creatures who must make their living by actively modifying their surroundings; in other words, people can only survive through labor. If one wishes to make a house, for example, one must assemble the necessary raw materials, be they animal skins, wooden planks, or gypsum drywall. If the process of production involves the use of machinery, these instruments must be provided with the fuel, lubricants, power supply, etc., which they need to operate.

Nevertheless, these various instruments and raw materials, if left to themselves, cannot produce anything of value. For a house to be produced, these components must be acted upon by human labor power. Indeed, the machinery and raw materials which are needed to produce the house are themselves merely the results of some prior expenditure of human labor power.

If we wish to exchange two commodities, say a chair and a sweater, we are faced with the difficulty of deciding what it is that makes them "equal". The chair and the sweater have differing use-values, they differ in form, size, weight, composition and structure. There would at first seem to be no way of comparing them, of making them in any way "equal" to each other.

Yet there is one relationship which these commodities share with all other commodities – each is the product of human labor, and each requires a definite amount of work, measured in hours, to produce from the natural materials available to that particular mode of production. And if all commodities can be compared according to the socially necessary amount of labor needed to produce them, exchange values can be directly related to this "labor value". A product requiring ten hours of labor to produce would be twice as valuable as one requiring only five hours.

This means that trading partners will seek to barter their commodities so that the labor values which are exchanged are equal. Suppose, for instance, that a chair requires fifteen hours of necessary labor time to produce, and a sweater requires five. The carpenter will not agree to exchange his chair for just one sweater, since he would then be trading his fifteen hours of labor for only five hours. It would then be more advantageous for him to expend five hours and make his own sweater. Therefore, chairs and sweaters will exchange at a rate of fifteen hours for fifteen hours—one chair will be "worth" three sweaters.

In the capitalist system of economic relationships, this value exchange is equal in every transaction except one—the capitalist's purchase of labor power as a commodity. It is within this exchange relationship, between the owner and the worker, that the appropriation of wealth by the capitalist takes place.

The sale of labor power as a commodity is the linchpin of capitalism. The capitalist, as the owner of capital, needs a supply of labor to carry out the actual manufacture of commodities. The workers, who own no capital, are forced to find some way to obtain the money they need to purchase exchange-values. As a result, the basic capitalist relationship is established—the workers sell their labor power to the capitalists and receive in turn a monetary wage, which they use to purchase their necessaries of life.

It is possible, then, to apply the labor value measurement to the sale of human labor power as a commodity. Indeed, it is within this commodity exchange that we find the secret of the bourgeoisie's dominant economic position.

Labor value consists of the number of hours socially necessary for the production of a commodity. In the case of human labor power as a commodity, the socially necessary time consists of the time spent to produce the food, shelter, clothing, etc., which allows the worker to make a living. In other words, the cost of labor power is the cost of providing the exchange-values which the worker purchases with the wages received from the capitalists.

All of these items can themselves be measured according to their labor values. Thus, the labor value of human labor power can be expressed in a definite socially necessary time. It may, for instance, take a socially necessary labor time of five hours to produce "one day's worth" of the worker's necessaries of life.

Under the simple commodity exchange, therefore, the worker would exchange five hours of labor for five hours of labor value. In other words, in five hours of working in the capitalist's factory, the worker would produce an amount of labor value equal to the day's wages received from the owner.

This relationship, however, does not take place under capitalism. Because the capitalists control the economy and the socio-political structure, they are able to compel the workers to exchange their labor power on terms which are unequal and favorable to the owners. Workers labor, not for the five hours of value they receive in wages, but for a full eight hour day. During this "extra" three hours, the workers continue to expend labor power and create value, but they receive nothing in exchange for it. This three hours of value is appropriated by the owner as "surplus value".

To the workers, it may appear as though nothing unusual has happened. They have agreed to work for one day and they have been paid for one day. Nevertheless, the fact remains that the value they have received in this exchange is much less than the value they have created and given to the capitalist. They have, in effect, given the owner eight hours of labor value in exchange for only five.

Since money is, in the capitalist scheme, the universal commodity which may be exchanged for any other commodity, we can also picture this process in monetary terms, which may make it more clear. Suppose that a clock in our economy is worth $45. A capitalist thus begins to manufacture clocks, and gathers in his factory the raw materials, machinery and laborers necessary to begin this process. Let us assume that the capitalist must gather $15 worth of raw materials and use up $3 in depreciation (wear and tear on the machinery) for each clock he produces, and that it takes the laborer one hour to produce each clock. If the worker is to make an acceptable living, she must receive $5 an hour in wages, and she agrees to sell her labor power to the capitalist for this price.

The value of the clock, we have already pointed out, is $45. To produce this commodity, the capitalist must invest a total of $18 in raw materials and equipment. Thus, the labor power of the worker has increased the value of $18 worth of materials into $45 worth of commodity. In other words, the worker has added $27 worth of labor value to the commodity. But, in exchange for this $27 worth of labor power, she receives only $5.

The difference between the labor value created by the worker and the value she is paid for her labor is the surplus value, which is appropriated by the capitalist once the commodities are sold. And, it can be readily seen, the surplus value is generated by the fact that the capitalist has not paid the worker for the full value of her labor power. In effect, the owner is able to force the worker to labor under the agreement, "I'll give you $5 if you give me $27."

In the capitalist economic apologia for this state of affairs, it is asserted that this surplus value is simply the share of wealth which goes to Capital, as "compensation" for the owner's "entrepreneurial skills" and as a "reward" for his "risk of capital".

It can be seen from our analysis that this is nonsense. While many capitalists do indeed perform some managerial tasks for which they are compensated, these tasks are entirely unconnected with the functioning of the capitalist production cycle. It is not necessary for the capitalist to be at all involved in the actual day-to-day running of his business; indeed, most capitalists simply hire professional managers to perform these tasks for them. Such capital-owners need not lift a finger to make their living—they simply hire workers and managers to produce wealth for them.

As for the bourgeois argument that they are "risking" their capital and deserve to be "rewarded", this too is nonsense, since the money that they risk was obtained precisely through the expropriation of their workers, by not paying the laborers for the full value of their work. It is the capitalist's money only by virtue of the fact that he controls the social relationships which allow him to appropriate it from the workers and prevent them from doing anything about it.

The capitalists do not have a monopoly on business skill or decision-making ability or any other economic quality. What they do have—and that which allows them to live off the labor of their workers—is a monopoly on capital. It is only the illusions of alienated bourgeois economics which prevents workers from seeing that the owning class is parasitical; it lives by allowing the working class to create wealth and then siphoning off most of that wealth for itself.

The relationship between the workers and the owners is thus inherently hostile and antagonistic. The interests of the working class are to eliminate the bourgeoisie's position of privilege and to keep the commodities it has produced for itself; the interests of the capitalists are to expropriate an ever-larger portion of the wealth created by the labor of the working class.

Further, as the relationship between bourgeoisie and proletariat is antagonistic, so too is the relationship between individual capitalists. Each capitalist has as his goal that of increasing his stock of capital for investment, allowing him to produce more labor value and appropriate an ever-growing amount of surplus value. The capitalist can only do this by exchanging his commodities to consumers and thus realizing their full exchange value. Thus, the relationship between capitalists is competitive, with each attempting to exchange commodities to consumers before the others can do the same.

This mutually antagonistic relationship leads to a steady change in the mode of production. At first, capitalist competition is characterized by a large number of small enterprises, none of which is able to exercise any great influence on the supply of commodities or on the labor time necessary to produce them. This is due to the fact that these relations are between owners who have only limited individual capitals, each unable to gain a significant advantage over the others.

The first change in this relationship comes as a result of the conglomeration of capital into the joint stock company or corporation. In this relationship, several individual capital owners agree to unify their capitals under a joint management. The resulting larger capital is able to invest and generate surplus value much more efficiently than the individual components of its capital could. Thus, smaller capitals become absorbed into larger capitals, and the system of relationships between small capitalists is transformed into relationships between huge conglomerates of capital, each of which is controlled and dominated by a small number of capital-owners.

In addition, the normal process of competition among smaller capitalists results in the failure of those enterprises which lose out in this competition. The capital of these failed enterprises is snapped up by competitors, who thus grow larger. An inevitable consequence of capitalist relationships, Marx concluded, was the gradual centralization of capital into fewer and fewer hands.

If this process of competition were allowed to reach its culmination, there would be eventually one victorious capitalist controlling each industry. Eventually, the entire mode of production would be monopolized by one huge corporate entity, whose control of capital would give it virtually absolute power over human society.

In reality, these relationships are changed by the capitalists long before this point is reached. As the process of competition becomes more and more deadly to the capitalists, their interests turn from that of taking over their competitor's capital to that of safe-guarding their own. As a result, the relationship between capitalists changes. Now, rather than continuing their economic warfare, the capitalist corporations agree to end direct price competition and their attempts to realize surplus value at the expense of other corporations, and instead agree to divide the market into cartels or trusts, which allow each member to realize its surplus value unmolested within its own particular territory or sphere of influence.

The rise of a de facto monopoly within each industry has a corresponding effect on the capitalist exchange system. According to capitalist ideology, the prices of commodities are determined by the interaction of the "supply" of a commodity and the "demand" for it, and this interaction takes place through the impersonal mechanism known as the "marketplace". In reality, this process is not at all impersonal; it is based directly on the social relationships embodied in the capitalist system.

We must remember that the value of a commodity in a capitalist economy is based on the socially necessary labor time needed to produce it, and that this is a function of the relationship between humans and their surroundings. Viewed in this manner, the capitalist marketplace can be seen as merely a social relationship which is capable of determining how much labor time is "socially necessary".

If the productive forces manufacture more commodities than consumers have a desire or ability to pay for (and on the whole when we speak of "consumers" we mean workers purchasing their necessaries of life), it is obvious that the labor value embodied in these commodities is "too high"; that is, more labor power was used to produce these commodities than was socially necessary. As a result, in the exchange relationship, only that portion of value which is socially necessary finds a consumer. The labor value of the unexchanged portion is "wasted" and is unrealizable as surplus value.

This has a profound effect on the capitalist commodity producer. If he is unable to realize the full exchange value of his commodities, he is unable to realize the full surplus value which he has extracted from his workers and which is embodied in these commodities. In some cases, inability to sell the commodity at its full value may mean the complete loss of surplus value and a corresponding loss of the owner's invested capital.

When the amount of labor time invested in commodities is lower than that which is socially necessary, i.e., when commodities are "underproduced", the situation is reversed. Now, the socially necessary labor value of these commodities is actually higher than that contained in the commodities, and they will exchange at a higher value than that embodied in them. Thus, the capitalist gains a "surplus" surplus value.

In the pre-monopolist competitive period of capitalism, no individual capitalist is able to greatly influence either the number of commodities produced or the number sold; thus commodities tend to fluctuate around their actual value. These fluctuations are caused by the effects of over- or under-investment of labor into commodity production, and take their final form in the exchange relationship between consumers and producers.

Within each capitalist industry, moreover, profit rates tended to move towards equality. This was a function of the small mobile capitals then being invested, and also of the relatively small productive forces which were then available. Thus, if profits were to become particularly high in one area, capital would flow into this sector as other capitalists moved to take advantage of the higher rate of return on their investment. This leads to over-production and difficulty in realizing surplus value. Thus, the tendency is for profit rates in all industries to level off at some average level.

This average rate of profit allows the capitalists to view the selling price of their commodities as the price they paid to have it produced (wages, materials and machinery) plus an additional amount which gives them the average rate of profit on their investment. Over-production or under-production of the commodity would then have the effect of lowering or raising the amount of surplus value which is actually realized through exchange.

Monopolistic corporations, however, are able to charge prices which are higher than the average rate of profit, and thus higher than their labor value. In competitive capitalism, if one producer sells his commodities at a higher-than-average rate of profit, either his competitors will sell closer to their cost production and thus undercut his price, or new capital will flow into the area and equalize the profit rate again. Monopolies and oligopolies, however, have agreed to give up the practice of price-cutting and under-selling; at the same time, the huge amounts of capital needed to compete with the corporate giants tends to shut out potential competitors. Thus, monopolistic corporations are free to set their prices, within certain restraints, as high above value as they wish.

By forming monopolistic corporations within the capitalist system, the bourgeoisie is actually altering the basic relationships of this system. In turn, changes in these social relationships modify the relationship between the workers and the owners. This, however, is a dialectical process. The working class, facing the same social framework, also takes steps to alter the worker-capitalist relationship.

For the capitalists, who are initially locked into a competitive relationship with each other, the need to combine into a cooperative corporation comes about from their need to maintain their role as capital-owners. For the working class, faced with an ever-increasing domination by a smaller number of capitalists, combination into a cooperative association becomes necessary in order to maintain at least a portion of influence in the worker-capitalist relationship. If workers do not organize, they become completely dominated by the owners. Thus, while the owners are driven to form corporate entities and cartels, the workers are equally driven to form associations and unions.

This process is greatly aided by the capitalist factory system, which necessitates a large number of workers gathered at one place, with their tasks divided so as to make it necessary for individual workers to labor in close cooperation with each other. Day to day realities demonstrate to the worker that the interests of the working class are not the same as those of the factory owners—the owners seek to decrease wages and thus increase profits, while the workers seek to increase wages.

The workers soon learn that, if they are to protect and further their interests, they must oppose the capitalists with weapons that are at least equal to their own. The most powerful working class tool, the workers learn, is organization and association—the labor union. And the most powerful weapon that can be used by the labor union, the most direct expression of working class power, is the strike.

In the beginning of the capitalist era, the workers' aims are limited. The working class is aware that its interests are opposed to those of the owners, but the introduction of a new system of social relationships is not yet a practical possibility. Thus, early working class actions take the form of limited actions to correct a single perceived injustice, to gain limited benefits and concessions within the limits of the established worker-owner relationship. Strikes are limited, single-industry or even single-factory affairs, with limited, short-term goals— i.e., refusal to work longer hours, repeal of a wage cut, etc.

As the organization of the working class grows, the infant trade unions begin to grow in power and influence. Industry-wide unions are formed, and these eventually join forces to form trade union confederations. As the power of organized labor grows, its goals become more assertive, more overtly aggressive. Now, instead of merely opposing wage cuts, the unions work actively for wage increases; instead of opposing the lengthening of the working day, the workers fight for a shorter day. The basic relationship between the worker and the owner is still unaltered—the goal of the working class is not yet the abolition of this relationship, but merely that of strengthening the bargaining position of the worker vis-a-vis the capitalist.

The capitalists, of course, see in these working class actions a threat to their uninterrupted appropriation of surplus value, and they unleash the full repressive forces of the state and the military to oppose the working class organizations. Strikes are ruthlessly broken; working class leaders are arrested, imprisoned or attacked. To attempt to counter this state repression, the working class begins to organize and fight in the political as well as the economic sphere—alongside the working class's economic organization, the trade union, grows its political arm, the labor party.

Thus, while the capitalists are forming monopolies and cartels, the workers are organizing trade unions and labor parties. At the same time, moreover, the growth of monopoly corporate capitalism produces yet another social relationship— that of the imperialist and the neo-colony.

The monopolists are driven to constantly expand their capital and to extract an ever-increasing amount of surplus value. In the early stages of capitalism, this expansion took place entirely within the borders of the capitalist's own home country, and sufficient surplus value could be extracted from the capitalist's own national proletariat.

As productive abilities expand under corporate capitalism, however, they come into sharper conflict with the finite size of the capitalist's home market, leading to the problem of chronic overproduction of commodities (i.e., an investment of social labor power which is consistently higher than that which can be consumed). The overproduction crisis causes grave problems for the capitalists, since it directly interferes with the realization of surplus value.

The effects of overproduction on capitalist social relationships will be discussed later. The important point to be made here is that the problem of overproduction is lethal for the capitalists, and they are forced to find a way to escape the situation. The corporate capitalist's solution to this problem is economic imperialism, which takes the form of the expansion of invested capital outside of the company's national borders.

The targets of the imperialist enterprise's predations are the non-industrialized nations commonly referred to as the "Third World". These nations, for a variety of historical and social reasons, never introduced the capitalist mode of production, and are still functioning under feudal-type social relationships. In those cases where a bourgeois class is in the process of developing, it is small, weak and incapable of defending its interests from the monopolist imperialists.

The Third World offers a huge supply of untapped raw materials and a large pool of cheap labor power for the monopolists, and the superior productivity of the larger corporate capital quickly overwhelms smaller indigenous capitalists, giving the corporate interests de facto control over the nation's economy and turning it into an economic neo-colony. Capital flows from the monopoly capitalists into the neo-colony for investment, and the huge surplus values which are thus generated flow back to the corporate coffers.

Capitalist ideologists claim that the presence of monopoly corporations in the Third World is "beneficial"; that the capitalist enterprises are "aiding the underdeveloped nation's economy" by "providing jobs for native peoples" and "helping them on the road to economic self-sufficiency". These claims are nonsense. The imperialist-colonial relationship is as exploitative and lopsided as the capitalist-worker relationship.

Surplus values generated in the neo-colonies can be absurdly high, since the disparity between the socially expected "standard of living" in the monopolist nation and the neo-colony can be huge. In the monopolist country, it may take a socially necessary labor time of five hours per day to produce the housing, food, clothing, etc., purchased by the worker's wages. In the neo-colony, however, the standard of living is much lower; consequently, to produce "one day's worth" of the worker's necessaries of life may take only two hours instead of five. Thus, in an eight-hour day, the worker in the neo-colony produces six hours of surplus value rather than the three which can be extracted in the monopolist's own country.

The international trade relationship between monopolists and neo-colonies also reflects the position of domination which the corporate states enjoy over the non-industrialized nations. As we have seen, the capitalist marketplace is but a social expression of the relationship between buyer and seller, and serves to determine how much labor time is "socially necessary" for the production of commodities. In the monopolist-colony relationship, however, labor values themselves are grossly lopsided in favor of the corporate monopolists.

In the non-industrialized nations, the amount of labor time which is necessary to produce commodities from natural materials will differ markedly from that needed in the industrial countries. In the neo-colony, it may take a native manufacturer five hours to produce 100 pounds of cotton yarn. The monopolist nation, however, with its mechanized means of production, may require only two hours of necessary labor time to produce the same 100 pounds.

If the native were to attempt to sell his cotton in the industrial nation's market, he will find that it exchanges, not for the five hours of labor value that he put into it, but at the two hours which are socially necessary in the industrial society. On the other hand, if the monopolist would sell his cotton yarn in the neo-colony, he can sell it for two hours of value. The native will find that his commodities are everywhere crowded out by the imperialist's cheaper commodities.

Furthermore, the monopolist finds that he can sell his yarn for four or five hours of value, rather than the two they contain, and still be competitive with the native manufacturer. The imperialists thus extract a "surplus" surplus value.

The neo-colony is thus a loser in the buying and in the selling. The realities of the relationship between the monopolists and the neo-colonies forces the native to sell his commodities to the monopolists for less than the value he has invested in them, and also compels him to pay more for the monopolist's commodities than they are worth.

The domination of the neo-colony by the imperialist has a profound effect on the social relationships within the neo-colony. The legal and state apparatus of the neo-colony is dominated by the interests of the foreign monopolists, who use it to safeguard their dominant position. Thus, the semi-feudal colonial state, headed by the large landholders which are typical of feudal relationships, finds its interests and existence are tied to the support of the imperialists. The native bourgeoisie is weak and divided, and finds itself given a choice between complete submission to the interests of the monopolists or its destruction by competition from the imperialists. The remainder of the population consists of agrarian peasants and tenant farmers who are exploited by the landholders, and of the proletariat who are exploited by the monopoly capitalists and the native bourgeoisie.

The interests of these classes are mutually antagonistic. The interests of the agrarian peasantry are to depose the landlords and to own their own land, but monopolist support for the landholding government makes this impossible. The interests of the proletariat are to organize into unions and labor parties to oppose exploitation by the native capitalists and the foreign monopolists. The bourgeoisie is divided and uncertain; part of it is tied to foreign financial interests and must support the puppet government, part wishes to depose the foreigners and install a native capitalist ruling class. Only the landlord class is completely supportive of the imperialists, since only monopolist economic and military intervention is able to save it from the wrath of the other classes.

In sum, the economic realities of the relationship between the monopolists and the neo-colonies forces the natives into opposition to the foreigners. This opposition, however, is influenced by the intensity of the imperialist-colonial relationship, which is fundamentally different from the worker-capitalist link. Within the capitalist mode of production, the worker is unable to function without the capitalist who buys his labor power. The neo-colony, however, was able to exist independently of the capitalists until they invaded and seized control. Thus, while the struggle of the working class is at this point limited to improving the position of the worker vis-a-vis the capitalists, the goal of the neo-colony from the outset is to smash this relationship, to expel the foreign monopolists from the country. Thus, while the goals of the working class are, in the beginning, reformist, the goals of the neo-colonies are from the outset revolutionary.

The social dynamics of the capitalist mode of production are thus multi-faceted and contradictory. The capitalists are in conflict with the workers, with each other, and with the neo-colonies. The interplay between these pairs of opposites are what Marx referred to as capitalism's "inner laws of motion".

As these social relationships change, however, they at the same time alter the way human society relates with its surroundings. Thus, the dialectical relations within capitalism transform and at the same time are transformed by material surroundings, producing a new relationship between human society and human surroundings. Through the dialectical process, Marx concluded, this relationship would eventually be altered to the point where the existing human social structure was no longer compatible with the fundamental task of human society—extracting the means of life from natural materials through human labor.

Since the social relationships which make up the capitalist mode of production are framed in economic terms and serve economic purposes, it is apparent that the first symptoms of incompatibility between capitalism and its surroundings will occur in the economic sphere; in the form of aberrations, conflicts and crises.

Such crises do occur in capitalism, and, while the capitalist economists are at a loss to explain these periodic upheavals, Marx, by laying bare the social relationships which underlie capitalist ideology, is able to present a clear picture of their origin and their ultimate destination.

The earliest forms of capitalist crises take place because of the atomistic, individualistic form of capitalist social relationships. The determination of socially necessary labor time is, as we have seen, made through the social mechanisms of the marketplace, which compares the labor time invested in the production of a commodity (supply) with the socially necessary amount of this commodity (demand).

In early competitive capitalism, however, the capitalist is forced to operate with little or no knowledge of either of these relationships. Because of the individualistic inter-capitalist relationship, the manufacturer has no way of knowing how much of a given commodity will be produced by competing capitalists, and thus has no way of knowing the total supply of the commodity he is producing. Similarly, since each capitalist provides only a small portion of the necessary supply of a given commodity, he has no way of determining how much production is socially necessary.

As a result, the capitalist system as a whole operates haphazardly. If the given supply happens to match the given demand — that is, if expended labor power matches the socially necessary amount of labor power — this is only due to the fortunes of pure chance. Capitalism has no rational way of matching production levels to those which are socially necessary. Far from being regulated efficiently by an "invisible hand", capitalist production is largely a hit-and-miss affair. As a result, the actual exchange values (prices) of commodities constantly fluctuate, as the capitalists continuously invest too much or too little labor power into commodity production.

In the absence of any planned method of regulating the social investment of labor power, each individual capitalist, driven by the imperative to realize surplus value and accumulate capital, responds by maximizing his own production in hopes of maximizing his surplus value. This, in turn, produces a tendency within the capitalist system for aggregate labor power to be invested at levels higher than those which are socially necessary—i.e., the supply consistently tends to run ahead of demand. This in turn leads to a drop in exchange value and a loss of surplus value.

In the early stages of capitalist development, this contradiction is not of great importance. With its rather limited productive capacity, the early capitalist system finds that population increases and other factors produce a rise in social demand that can keep pace with expanding productive ability. The capitalists also find that the surplus value which has been capitalized and reinvested in new productive ability will re-enter the economy as wages for the sector of the economy which produces these "capital goods", thus tending to pull total demand into par with total supply.

As productive levels increase, however, the "overproduction crisis" becomes more and more dangerous for the capitalists. In classical capitalist economics ("Say's law"), total demand is always assumed to be capable of absorbing the total supply, since the "costs" paid out by businesses are in fact "incomes" for other businesses. The high productivity of the monopolist system, however, combined with huge surplus values, upsets this ideal situation.

As the monopolists increase their profits and income, their demand for commodities does not increase at the same rate. At the same time, the ability to turn out an ever-increasing number of commodities expands rapidly. As a result, the monopolist economy continually tends to produce more commodities than the market can absorb—a "demand crunch". The monopolists find that a large portion of their commodities are "socially unnecessary"—that is, they cannot be exchanged and their surplus value cannot be realized.

Faced with a glutted market, the monopolists see that the normal rate of profit cannot be made, and cut back on the amount of money that is reinvested as capital. In essence, this money is taken out of capital circulation. New investment falls, plants are closed down, employees are laid off—all the hallmarks of a recession.

The only way out of this situation, within the context of capitalist relations, is to increase the share of value which is received by the working class, and thus to increase the ability of the working class to absorb the overproduction of commodities. This, however, presents an entirely different threat to the capitalist.

As we have seen, the basis for the capitalist's surplus value lies in the fact that the workers do not receive the full value of the commodities which they produce. This is a "zero-sum" relationship—if the share of total value going to the workers is increased, the share of value which goes to the capitalists must necessarily decrease, and vice versa. Thus, increasing the share of value which goes to the worker, in the form of wages and benefits, directly decreases the value expropriated by the capitalists in the form of profits. Increasing labor's share of value from five hours a day to six directly reduces the surplus value appropriated by the capitalists from three hours to two.

Thus, rather than being led out of the overproduction crisis, the capitalists find themselves forced into an entirely different set of circumstances which produces the very same effect—a direct drop in the production and accumulation of surplus value. The capitalist is caught between the horns of an insoluble contradiction—in order to escape the crisis of overproduction, which lowers his accumulation of surplus value) he must raise the share of value going to labor, yet this also has the direct effect of lowering his accumulation of surplus value.

This conflict is inevitable so long as production continues to center around exchange-value rather than use-value, and so long as one class of society appropriates the surplus value created by another. In other words, it will continue so long as there is private accumulation of capital.

For these conditions to be obliterated, however, it is necessary to bring about a complete change in the mode of production. Rather than private accumulation of capital through the production of exchange-values, the new mode of production must take the form of social investment of capital, in such a manner that social investment is rationally and deliberately matched with the current demand, through a system of allocation based on the distribution of use-values. These are the basic hallmarks of a socialist mode of production, and they are made necessary by capitalism's inability to meet these needs.

Since the capitalist mode of production is unable to solve these inherent crises rationally, they are solved irrationally. Periods of expansion within the capitalist economy tend to produce trends of overproduction and a rise in wage levels. Both of these trends interfere with the appropriation of surplus value (or, in the terms of classical economics, they produce a fall in the rate of profit).

As profit rates fall, capitalists respond by cutting back on their investments of capital and by idling their productive capacity. The result is falling prices, increased layoffs and unemployment, and falling profit rates — in other words, a recession.

As productive capacity is thus cut back, the supply of commodities falls to match the current level of demand, thus returning the profit rate to its "normal" level. Capital is reinvested, production expands and the cycle starts all over again.

This is the source of the capitalist "business cycle", the continual up and down flow of boom and bust. These cycles of expansion and contraction, it can now be seen, are the inescapable effects of capitalist social relationships; they are not the accidental results of incompetent or incorrect decisions made by businessmen, or government interference. They are intrinsic to the capitalist mode of production, and cannot be avoided or reversed within the context of capitalist social relationships.

With each new portion of the cycle, moreover, the process reinforces itself. During each new "expansion", the level of productive forces and their productivity tends to increase. Consequently, with each "depression" a successively larger and larger portion of this social productive capacity must be idled to alleviate the effects of the overproduction crisis. Also, a continual increase in productive ability means that the market can be saturated more quickly, leading to the onset of the overproduction problem at successively lower levels of the economy's capacity. In the United States in the early 1980's—a "boom" time in the cycle—the economy was functioning at only 75% of its capacity.

Thus, the tendency for late monopoly capitalism is to continually fall to lower and lower levels of productive capacity, idling an ever-growing portion of machinery and labor power. Idleness, unemployment and depression, far from being an "aberration" in a capitalist economy, can now be seen as the normal state of monopoly production.

Under these conditions, the relationship between the monopolist imperialists and the economic neo-colonies takes on an increasingly larger role in the Marxian description of the capitalist mode of production.

Although the expansion of capital into the neo-colonies has always been important for the monopolists, it become particularly vital since the effects of the overproduction crisis have begun to make themselves felt. The imperative is simple; if the monopolist is to avoid the effects of saturating the market through overproduction, that market must be expanded.

In the initial stages of economic imperialism, the capitalists utilize their overseas neo-colonies as sources of raw materials and cheap labor. Under the effects of overproduction, however, the neo-colony is turned more and more into a "captive market", into which the capitalists can exchange commodities which would go unsold in their own countries.

Of course, in order to exchange more and more commodities with the neo-colony, the value which goes to the neo-colony's workers, in the form of wages, must grow, so that they can afford to buy what the capitalists have to sell. This has the effect of lowering the rate of surplus value in the neo-colonies. However, for the monopolist struggling with the effects of the overproduction crisis, the short-term benefits are worth the long-term drop in profit rates.

In the long run, however, the monopolists are doomed. Try as they might, they cannot construct a new planet. Since the Earth is of finite and limited size, the market for the monopolists' commodities is finite and limited also. The expansion of the monopolists' productive ability to literally global proportions will only mean that the overproduction crisis will begin to assert itself on global scales instead of merely national. The entire world economy will find itself subjected to the chronic depression and stagnation which are typical of monopoly capitalism.

The increase in the share of value which goes to the neo-colony (in the form of wages and other payments which enable the colonials to purchase the monopolists' commodities) strengthens the position of the neo-colonies vis-a-vis the imperialists. The class clashes within the neo-colony grow sharper as the economic position of the native purchasers grows more powerful. The neo-colony sees for the first time the possibility of breaking ties with the imperialist power and becoming politically and economically independent.

As we have noted earlier, the classes within the neo-colony who have interests opposed to those of the imperialists are the workers, the peasantry, and a portion of the native capitalists. To this list must also be added the so-called "petty bourgeoisie", which is composed of artisans, professional intellectuals, managers and small shop owners who must perform part of their own labor.

In the neo-colonies, opposition to imperialism is inevitable, driven by the nature of its social relationships. Since the governmental apparatus of the neo-colony is controlled by imperialist interests, the opposition classes of the neo-colony cannot win concessions through the political sphere. And since they are not free to organize economic associations or unions to increase their influence, they cannot make use of economic struggle. The revolutionary tensions within the neo-colony, therefore, can find only one method of expression and only one path to success—armed insurrection. If the imperialist grip on the neo-colony is to be cast off, it is necessary for the neo-colony to rise up, weapons in hand, and pry the imperialist hands from its throat

THREE:
Fundamentals of Leninism

Marx himself died in 1883, before the process of economic imperialism had gotten fully underway. As a result, his writings on the imperialist-colonial relationship are scanty and incomplete. It fell to later generations of Marxists to study this relationship. After Marx's death, his thought was adopted and codified by a group of German socialists who formed a new international organization to propagate them, the Second International.

As we have seen, Marx's philosophical framework was one of dialectical totality, in which things were composed of interpenetrating and co-determining facets. Marx criticized the materialists for asserting that matter was the "cause" of all actions, and likewise attacked the idealists for claiming that ideas produced all human actions. While social reality was influenced by the ideas of humanity, Marx pointed out, those ideas were themselves the products of social reality. As Engels writes, "Reciprocal action is the true *causa finalis* of things. We cannot go back further than to knowledge of this reciprocal action, for the very reason that there is nothing behind to know."

The descriptions and definitions which Marx gives for this interpenetrating process are, however, difficult to understand in a social framework which views the relationships of things linearly, in a one-to-one causal relationship. Therefore, after Marx's death, those socialists who were unable to grasp the Marxian concept of dialectical totality took it upon themselves to modify, simplify and re-define Marxism. This new conception has been called "dialectical materialism", "historical materialism" or "economic determinism"; all terms which Marx himself never used.

The socialists of the Second International, faced with a decline in militant working class activity, were forced to focus their attention on the development of revolutionary theory. In the absence of an organized revolutionary movement, the German socialist movement became more and more divorced from reality, and eventually reduced all of Marx's profound insights into the simple formula, "Material economic conditions determine consciousness." In other words, these theorists concluded, Marxism was a positive science which described and analyzed the objective laws of human development just as Newton had studied physics and Darwin had studied biology. According to these "scientific Marxists", Marxism asserted that prevailing economic conditions directly determined all of the rest of societal organization, including the religious, political, legal and ethical spheres, and that the actions of the economic sphere were automatic and eternal, unaffected by human wishes or desires.

Thus, according to this "economic determinist" view, human development is brought about by the action of economics, and this motion is determined by regular and predictable natural laws which humans are powerless to avoid or escape. The economic base directly determines and controls the social superstructure which is built upon it.

In the beginning, Leninism started its life as a criticism of the Second International, which, led by Kautsky, had reduced Marxism to an historical inevitability. Lenin rejected this conception, and argued that no socialist revolution could ever occur unless workers actively organized and fought for it. While expressly rejecting philosophical idealism, Lenin brought a much larger voluntaristic trend to Marxism than had Kautsky.

When the Leninists looked at the socialist movement as it existed shortly before World War I, however, it saw only a reformist Social Democratic Party—the militant revolutionary movement was small, weak and cut off from the masses of working people. In order to explain why the workers were unwilling to embrace revolutionary communism, the Leninists turned to the notion of "false consciousness"; the working class rejection of communism is caused by a "false ideology" imposed upon them by the bourgeoisie and by the reactionary Social Democrats who had led them down the path of liberal reformism. The capitalists had succeeded in corrupting the working class movement, infecting it with a "false consciousness" which hid from the workers their "real" interests. Lenin concluded that ideological corruption by the bourgeoisie had removed the revolutionary potential of the working class.

Lenin opined:

> The history of all countries shows that the working class, exclusively by its own efforts, is able to develop only trade union consciousness, i.e., the conviction that it is necessary to combine in unions, fight the employers, and strive to compel the government to pass necessary labor legislation, etc.

The Leninists thus introduced a new strategy into the socialist movement; the workers would obtain their revolutionary consciousness by having it brought to them by a dedicated core of communist theorists, by "professional revolutionaries":

I assert: (1) that no revolutionary movement can endure without a stable organization of leaders maintaining stability, (2) that the broader the popular mass drawn spontaneously into the struggle, which forms the basis of the movement and participates in it, the more urgent the need for such an organization, and the more solid this organization must be (for it is much easier for all sorts of demagogues to side-track the more backward sections of the masses), (3) that such an organization must consist chiefly of persons engaged in revolution as a profession, (4) that in an autocratic state, the more we confine the membership of such an organization to professional revolutionaries who have been trained in the art of combating the political police, the more difficult it will be to unearth this organization, and (5) the greater will be the number of people from the working class and from the other social classes who will be able to join the movement and perform active work in it.

Lenin's philosophical base, therefore, asserted that human society was governed by "objective economic laws". These laws, however, could be comprehended by the trained elite of professional revolutionaries (the Communist Party), and human society could thus be guided by these professionals in accordance with the "laws of the dialectic".

The Marxist-Leninist Third International took this notion of "economic determinism" to its logical conclusion. The Leninists asserted that (1) Marxism describes the natural laws which govern the development of human society, (2) Trained Marxist-Leninists are able to interpret these laws and thus to predict the future development of human society, and (3) the party of trained Marxist-Leninists should therefore be allowed to rule over society to insure that it is guided, according to these "natural laws", down the inevitable path to socialism.

Rather than a Marxian interrelationship between theory and action, Lenin developed the new notion of "reflective knowledge". According to Lenin, all knowledge and theory is but a reflection of existing economic circumstances, and no theory can be considered valid unless it is tested against existing economic reality. Human society was a "superstructure" which was dependent on the economic "base", a base which was altered according to immutable laws of development.

In his economic writings, Lenin on the whole adhered to the "classical Marxist" description already set out in the last chapter, although, in accordance with his determinist viewpoint, he largely ignored the role of social relationships in bringing about these economic factors. Lenin accepted that capitalism was in a state of crisis over the overproduction problem, and saw that the exploitation of the neo-colonies was vital to saving the imperialists, at least temporarily, from this fate. In fact, Lenin pointed out, in the early 20th century, Russia was the largest and most thoroughly exploited of the neo-colonies.

The fundamental principles of Leninist revolutionary practice are derived from this philosophical and ideological framework. Since monopoly capitalism is a worldwide system with global connections, each part of the imperialist system is linked integrally with the rest of the network. Thus, it becomes possible to attack monopoly capitalism at its weakest points – in the neo-colonies. In the capitalist nations, Lenin asserted, the working class had become sidetracked in a futile effort to organize unions and win economic goals such as higher wages. The proletariat in these countries, according to Lenin, had given up the goal of fighting the capitalists and now sought only to live more comfortably within the capitalist system.

By contrast, Lenin pointed out, relations between the neo-colonies and the imperialists were antagonistic and hostile, and the colonial-imperialist relationship was revolutionary rather then merely reformist. Therefore, Lenin concluded, the center of socialist revolution could be shifted from the industrialized working class to the neo-colonial peasants and workers. Lenin asserted that it had become possible for the backward neo-colonies, particularly Russia, to be led by the Party to carry out an anti-capitalist revolution, shatter the world monopolist network, and introduce socialism.

By asserting this unorthodox view, Lenin quickly made himself an outcast among the international Marxist movement. The remaining Second International Marxists, including the Russian Menshevik faction, argued that the conditions for the defeat of capitalism could only exist in the developed bourgeois nations of Europe, not in backward, feudalist Russia. Conditions in Russia, the orthodox Marxists believed, were suitable only for an anti-feudal revolution that would introduce the capitalist republic, as it had in Europe centuries before.

The Russian Bolsheviks, led by Lenin and Trotsky, rejected the Menshevik analysis. The Second International socialists, they concluded, had not examined the struggle between the imperialist monopolists and their neo-colonies, and thus had little understanding of the monopolist-colonial relationship. It was to the credit of Lenin and Trotsky that they studied these links and began to explore their implications.

The clearest theory of this relationship was developed by Trotsky and echoed by Lenin—the doctrine of "permanent revolution". According to Trotsky, the development of a capitalist sector in the neo-colonial economy (even though it was dominated by the capital of foreign monopolists) meant that feudal relations were in fact the immediate target of the Russian anti-colonial revolution. But because the native bourgeoisie was so dominated by the foreigners, Trotsky asserted, the Russian merchant class was too weak to make its own revolution. It therefore fell upon the peasants and the workers, the other two major anti-imperialist classes in the neo-colonies, to carry out the anti-feudal revolution under their own leadership.

A working class revolution carried out in the name of anti-feudalism, however, could not long remain within such limited goals. The working class, aided by the peasantry, would immediately turn the anti-feudal revolution into an anti-capitalist one. In other words, the workers would lead the "bourgeois" revolution, but would immediately turn it into the socialist revolution.

Faced with this example of the mortality of capitalism, Trotsky assumed, the working classes of the industrialized capitalist nations would rise in rebellion and install socialist regimes in their own countries. Thus, the revolution in Russia would become permanent—it would continue uninterrupted from the anti-feudal rebellion to the worldwide socialist revolution.

Lenin then turned his considerable organizational talents to the question of practical revolutionary action—how to organize and bring about the triumph of such a permanent revolution? In Europe, the working class movement had relative freedom to operate; it could disseminate its point of view through leaflets and newspapers, it could organize rallies and meetings, it could participate in the electoral process.

In Russia, however, none of these options existed. The Tsarist bureaucracy crushed dissent with its Okhrana political police, its censorship apparatus and its Cossack troopers. Lenin thus concluded that any revolutionary organization in Russia had to exist completely underground and live a conspiratorial, secret existence. To survive under conditions of repression, the revolutionary party had to live under strict military discipline within a rigid pyramidical leadership and command structure.

In addition, Lenin asserted, the revolutionary party must serve as the "defenders of the faith", as interpreter of the impersonal "laws" of dialectical materialism. Left to themselves, Lenin asserted, the working class would only develop the mentality and outlooks of reformism. They would forever fight for higher wages and a more equitable worker-capitalist relationship, and would never come to see that the capitalist mode must be smashed and replaced by a socialist one. Lenin therefore declared that the party must serve as the educators of the working class; it had to keep the principles of socialism and fight in the interests of the workers.

It seems likely that, had the Russian Revolution in 1917 actually produced a worldwide socialist upheaval, Lenin may have been vindicated. The failure of the Russian Revolution (and every Leninist revolution since) lies precisely in the fact that the working class was not "provoked" to revolution, leaving the former neo-colony to face the awesome tasks of attempting to construct a socialist mode of production in a backward economy that was not equipped to support socialism.

On several occasions, anti-colonial revolutionists had attempted to win independence from foreign domination (Mexico in 1910, Ireland in 1916-1921). But, having conquered political power, they found that they were unable to support themselves economically. The industrialized foreigners quickly re-established their economic domination and transformed the country into a neo-colony once again.

The only way to prevent this is to rapidly build up an economic infrastructure within the neo-colony, both to allow for economic independence and to build up a military force to defend the ex-colony from further imperialist predations. Each of these necessities are in turn dependent upon the strength of the ex-colony's productive ability, which is a function of its level of industrialization.

In the capitalist nations, industrialization had been accomplished over a long period of time by the rise of the capitalists and their factory method of production. This industrial capacity allowed the bourgeoisie, aided by the peasantry and the infant working class, to overwhelm and overthrow the feudal mode of production.

The root cause of the Leninist revolution in the neo-colonies is this urgent need to throw off the twin restrictions of a semi-feudal economic system and the domination of foreign capital. Since this process cannot be carried out peacefully in a neo-colony, it could be accomplished only by a revolution, by a social upheaval that destroyed the old order of things.

While the destruction of the feudal order had been carried out in the European countries by the rising bourgeoisie, allied with the peasantry and the proletariat. This pattern, however, had been rendered impossible in Russia and all other neo-colonies by the near-total domination of the native economy by the foreign monopolists. Imperialist domination laced the neo-colony with a web of restrictions that systematically drained it of wealth and resources, at the same time crippling the growth of a native merchant class and indigenous industry.

The Russian Revolution at first followed the path that had been trodden by the European bourgeoisie. When the Tsarist system tottered and fell, power passed to the infant Russian bourgeoisie in the form of the Kadet party and the Provisional Government. The Russian bourgeoisie, however, had been so weakened by the external domination of the monopolists and the internal opposition of the peasants and workers that it could have only a tenuous grip on power. It had destroyed the old feudal relations (or at least had played a role in their destruction), but it proved unable to substitute capitalist relations in their place. The economic growth and industrialization which circumstances demanded was quite beyond the ability of the native bourgeoisie to provide.

As a result, power passed to the organized party of the Russian peasant, the nominally socialist Trudovik party headed by Kerensky. The Trudoviks no longer represented the direct interests of the Russian merchant class, but they proved to be equally unable to provide the rapid industrialization that was needed or to halt the foreign domination of the country. Russia seemed to be on the verge of falling, as had the Mexican revolution, back into the neo-colonial fold of imperialism.

It was at this point, however, that the Russian Revolution took a direction different from any other revolution in history. The cause of that deviation was the unique social and organizational outlook known as Leninism.

Since the bourgeoisie had, under the Kadets, proven itself to be incapable of solving the problems of industrialization and economic independence, Lenin concluded that he had been correct in supposing that the Russian capitalists were unable to make their own revolution, and that it therefore fell upon the working class and the peasantry to do this. In the October Revolution, Lenin seized power from the Trudoviks and triumphantly waited for the worldwide socialist revolution to follow. He waited until he died in 1924.

During the period preceding Lenin's death, the social and class structure of Russia was confused. The peasants still clamored for title to their land, and the working class embraced Lenin's socialist vision. The Bolshevik faction, however, now known as the Communist Party, was composed largely of members of the petty bourgeoisie; professionals and intellectuals. With the death of Lenin and the rise of Stalin, the class structure of the Leninist system soon became apparent.

The failure of the worldwide revolution left the newly-formed Soviet Union surrounded by hostile imperialist powers. At the same time, the economically undeveloped USSR lacked the means to defend her independence or to build an independent economy. It therefore fell to Stalin and his petty-bourgeois Party to build what he referred to as "socialism in one country".

The Stalinist bureaucracy had to meet several requirements before it could carry out this task. Since the bourgeoisie had already proven itself incapable of solving the problems of economic independence, the class that carried out this task had to be anti-capitalist and anti-bourgeois in its ideological outlooks. Since Russian independence had been and was being threatened by foreign domination, this ruling class had to be anti-imperialist in its policy towards the capitalist nations. And, since a process of industrialization through market-spurred competition would have at best proven too slow and at worst would have allowed the return of foreign economic domination, the new ruling class had to advocate a non-market centrally-planned model of economic organization. By 1924, the Communist Party in the Soviet Union demonstrated all of these characteristics.

The Leninist bureaucratic state is, therefore, only nominally socialist. The process of Leninist revolution does not describe the transition from capitalism to socialism; it describes instead the transition from feudalism to state capitalism. In its historical context, the Leninist mode of production is the result of a tottering feudal system and a rising capitalist system which is too weak to take its place. Under these circumstances, if society is to continue to extract its means of life from its surroundings, a new mode of production must be introduced, but the capitalist mode which served this purpose in Europe cannot be constructed.

The "historical task" of the Leninist regime, therefore, is to complete the tasks of mechanization and industrialization of the means of production which had been accomplished by the bourgeoisie in the West, but which capitalism is unable to complete (or even begin) in the neo-colonies.

Leninist revolutions, then, despite the propaganda to the contrary, are not and cannot be internationalist revolts on behalf of the working class. They are in essence a variety of "revolutionary nationalism", a method of freeing the neo-colony from foreign domination. They are fought in the interests of the national petty bourgeoisie allied with the workers and the peasants.

It is beyond the scope of this work to give a detailed analysis of the social and economic relationships which underlie the "Leninist mode of production". We can instead briefly summarize these relations by pointing out that, in Leninist state capitalism, the ruling class establishes a position of dominance by its collective bureaucratic control of the state and economic apparatus. The Leninist "state capitalist" economy works by extracting a surplus from the peasantry and using this to invest in industrial production, which in turn extracts a surplus from the workers. This produces a steady flow of wealth to the collective ruling class. The collectivization of agriculture and the centrally-commanded industrial program are relationships of exploitation.

The programs undertaken by the Leninist state quickly industrialize the economy and allow society to once again extract its living from existing surroundings. As this requirement is fulfilled, however, a new system of social relationship becomes necessary. In other words, the Leninist mode of production begins to exhibit contradictions which indicate that it has outlived its usefulness and must be replaced.

Examination of the Leninist mode of production will show that these contradictions arise in the form of a new set of social relationships which develop within it — the mediation of a new class of factory managers and enterprise executives between the workers and the centralized state command apparatus. The relationship between the factory managers and the central state becomes more and more important as these contradictions develop, and as the power of the decentralized managers comes into sharper conflict with the planning bureaucracy.

These relationships are the product of a trend in the Leninist economies to underproduce consumer-oriented commodities and to overproduce capital-oriented commodities. These contradictions produce a tendency towards decentralization, in which the local factory managers must be given an increasing share of economic decision-making power. The factory managers come to take more and more the role of an individual controller of capital.

The Leninist state attempted to maintain its dominant position over these new managers with the introduction of *perestroika*, or "restructuring". *Perestroika* was nothing more than an attempt by the Leninist bureaucrats to introduce the decentralization which the economy demands while at the same time keeping it under control — to grant the local factory managers freedom of action, but only within narrowly-defined limits, i.e., in such a way that it did not threaten the interests of the ruling class.

This attempt failed, and the Leninist bureaucracy collapsed from its own weight. Economic conditions now demand that the lower levels of the economic apparatus, the enterprise managers, will assume de facto control of the economy and its social relationships. The Leninist state falls and is replaced by a series of capitalist republics.

In this way, Lenin's unsuccessful socialist revolution has, like the Mexican revolution, fallen back into the capitalist fold.

The capitalist economists and politicians who are happily declaring the "end of socialism", however, are missing the point. The downfall of the Leninist mode of production did not occur because it "didn't work" — rather, it fell precisely because it *did* work, and accomplished the changes in social relationships which were demanded by circumstances, i.e., it industrialized the means of production. The "historical role" of the Leninist regime had been completed, and it fell to a system which is better suited for carrying out the next "task".

But the process of Leninist revolution is not likely to disappear. The Leninist mode of production is perfectly suited to the needs of a neo-colony that is able to throw off the yoke of the imperialists and build an independent economy. This leads to the probability that, even after the collapse of "Leninism" in Russia and China, other nations will follow the Leninist path of development.

Obviously, a nation is capable of building an independent economy only if it has access to the necessary natural and human resources. So far, Leninist revolutions have occurred only in large countries with a wealth of such resources (Russia and China) or in countries which were supported by these larger countries (Cuba, Korea, Vietnam).

There are still, however, large neo-colonies which have the potential to construct an independent industrial infrastructure if they can throw off the stranglehold of the monopolists. Among these nations are India, Brazil, Chile and Mexico. All of these nations are making efforts to industrialize their economy, and all of these efforts are dominated by foreign capital.

The smaller nations which have attempted anti-colonial revolutions (El Salvador, Nicaragua, Venezuela, Bolivia) do not have sufficient internal resources with which to construct an independent industrial base. They are dependent for these on other nations, and can at best merely trade economic dependence on one power bloc for dependence on another.

As those neo-colonies which are capable of making the Leninist transition do so, the process of Leninist revolution will come to an end. When it is over, the Leninist mode of production will disappear, and the world will once again consist solely of rival monopolist blocs and their neo-colonies. Capitalist relations will once again rule the globe, and capitalist crises will reach their crescendo.

FOUR:

Transition to Socialism

The failure of the Leninist neo-colonials to bring about a socialist transformation in their countries forces modern revolutionaries in the industrialized nations to reflect carefully on this experience. By studying the reasons for Lenin's successes and his failures, we can derive valuable lessons to be applied to our own contemporary situation.

In accordance with Marxian dialectics, our ideas and theories about social relations must be grounded in, and in unity with, existing circumstances. At the same time, our ideas and theories are a part of those circumstances and can be used to alter them. The first step in formulating a revolutionary program for our time is, therefore, a consideration of existing social relationships and how our theories and actions can affect them.

As we have already noted, late monopoly capitalism is in a perpetual state of crisis. It cannot escape the twin dilemmas of overproduction and decline in the rate of surplus accumulation. Existing social relationships inexorably force the capitalists to expand the market for their commodities into the neo-colonies, allowing them a temporary reprieve from the ravages of overproduction.

This is only a temporary expedient, however. Once each monopolist bloc has staked out its claim in the neo-colonies, these "spheres of influence" will be saturated as surely as the imperialist's own home market. At this point, it becomes necessary for new markets to be seized, and, in the absence of any new territory to be conquered, this can only be done by taking the neo-colonies which are already claimed by other monopolists.

If the process is left to run its course, one imperialist power will eventually come to dominate the rest of the world and transform the globe into its neo-colony. The restless process of capital accumulation will, however, just as surely grow to saturate this global market, and the effects of overproduction will be felt on a global scale.

As economic capacity and productivity continue to grow under monopoly capitalism, moreover, profound changes are introduced into capitalist social relationships. Of increasing importance is the social structure which determines exchange value, the marketplace, which is crucial to the bourgeois mode of production.

In early capitalism, when the productive ability of society is relatively low, the general level of social production is insufficient to produce all of the various commodities which are necessary and desirable. This leads to a scarcity of commodities, and the task of the capitalist marketplace, as bourgeois ideology sees it, is to "allocate" these resources, to decide through the "impersonal marketplace" who will receive the scarce commodities and who will not. The capitalist marketplace bases this on the control of wealth—those with more wealth get more commodities. This is a convenient exchange system for a ruling class that controls most of society's wealth, and obtains it by siphoning it from the working class.

As productive abilities continue to expand under monopoly capitalism, however, the problem of "scarcity" becomes less and less acute. As commodities become overproduced, the capitalist exchange relationship becomes less suited to the social distribution of the necessities of life. When the supply of a commodity is scarce, potential consumers must compete with each other to get it, and the criterion for this competition is how much exchange value one is willing and able to part with.

If there is an abundant supply of the commodity available, however, the need for exchange-value competition disappears. Social circumstances now demand a system of distribution based on the allocation of resources according to use-value. Instead of determining whether this or that party to the social relationship will obtain the limited supply of commodities, the new system of distribution must determine the most efficient manner to distribute abundant supplies between both parties.

Thus, the affluence of the monopoly capitalist's high level of productivity undercuts the very basis for the capitalist's domination of social relationships, and forces profound changes in the mode of production. It demands, in essence, the production and distribution of use-values, not exchange-values.

The capitalist mode of production, which is by its very nature constructed around the private production of exchange-values (and the consequent appropriation of surplus value) is unable to adapt itself to the changes demanded by these circumstances. The result is an insoluble conflict — if humans are to continue to extract their means of life from existing circumstances through labor, the methods by which this process is carried out (i.e., the existing mode of production) must be altered drastically; yet capitalism is unable to adapt itself to these circumstances.

The resolution of this conflict is inescapable — the existing mode of production has begun to outlive its usefulness, and must be abandoned in favor of a more appropriate mode of production. In other words, the capitalist system must be destroyed and replaced by the socialist system.

In fighting to save themselves from this fate, the monopoly capitalists daily prove that they are no longer suited for providing the necessaries of life to the members of human society. The development and utilization of human productive capacity which is demanded by current circumstances is instead hampered and distorted by the narrow class interests of the bourgeoisie, who are forced to periodically cut back on the utilization of human productive forces in order to avoid producing more commodities than they can sell profitably.

The capitalist is not at all concerned with the production of use-values; he cares only about exchange-values, and is thus forced to lower the utilization of productive abilities which could otherwise be used to raise the standard of living for all members of human society. Instead of a self-managed super-abundant system which uses human labor power for everyone's benefit, monopoly capitalism produces a system in which human labor power is deliberately *underutilized* to protect the privileged position of the ruling class; a system which, instead of producing enough food to feed hungry people, uses "price supports" to pay farmers *not* to grow food and thus protects profit levels.

As the contradictions between social needs and capitalist needs grows, the social relationships within capitalism will come into increasingly sharper conflict. The workers of the industrialized nations will find themselves sinking deeper and deeper into relative poverty and stagnation, as the monopolists are forced to cut back on production to protect their profits. In the neo-colonies, the population continues to become poorer as wealth and surplus value continue to flow out of the country and into the imperialist's coffers.

The interests of the exploited workers and the exploited neo-colonials are the same. Both are dependent upon the full utilization of human productive ability to lift them out of their poverty and allow them to obtain their necessaries of life. Yet, the social necessity of full utilization is made impossible by capitalist social relations, and by the fact that control over these productive resources is monopolized by a handful of private capital owners.

Slowly but certainly, existing social relationships will force the working class to move from their former position of "trade union reformism", of strengthening their position in the worker-owner relationship, to that of revolution, of shattering the worker-owner relationship and abolishing the sale of human labor as a commodity. From "higher wages", the battle cry becomes "abolish the wage system".

In most of the industrialist nations (particularly in the United States) the monopolists have been able to avoid the dangers of a worker-colonial alliance by using their own respective relationships with these groups to drive a wedge between them. By consistently exporting capital to the neo-colonies and taking advantage of the lower wage rates there, the monopolists are able to establish a direct threat to their own workers. The monopolist country's working class, still locked within the context of the worker-owner relationship, views this export of jobs as a weakening of their position versus the capitalists. To these workers, the wage-earners in the neo-colonies come to be seen as the "enemy", as competitors who are "costing us jobs". The capitalists, in turn, are able to extract concessions from workers by threatening them with runaway plants and job losses.

The trade union organizations, organized as they are along narrow national lines, are powerless to fight this threat, and are reduced to the ignominious task of "negotiating" concessions which will allow a portion of union members to keep their jobs (at least until the next round of give-backs). Rather than fighting this international "whipsawing", the unions have become mouthpieces for the company, and echo the employers' cry for protectionist legislation that restricts the import of low-wage goods. The American auto and steel unions, with their "Buy American" campaign, are the most obvious examples. This does nothing more than divide workers of one country against workers of another, and strengthens the position of the capitalists over *all* of the workers. This is aided by the proliferation of international "free trade" agreements such as GATT and NAFTA, which allow capital to move freely between nations, while avoiding areas where worker strength is an obstacle.

So long as labor remains organized along narrow nationalist lines and views the workers of other countries as enemies, it will be unable to fight the international organizations of capital, with its vast financial networks and its multinational corporations. Given that capital is free to move its resources across national boundaries anytime it chooses, labor can only fight back if it is equally powerful internationally. In short, circumstances demand the establishment of an international labor movement, a multinational working class organization which can fight the international monopolists on any turf they choose. Until this is done, the monopolists will continue to enjoy the ability to utilize the colonials against the workers, and thus to increase their power over both.

Militant unions such as the IWW have always called for international labor solidarity, but now the mainstream labor unions are being forced into a similar position. The United Mine Workers of America once signed an agreement with coal unions in England, Germany, South Africa and Australia which pledges to expand global cooperation and joint initiatives. The ultimate goal, UMWA organizers said, was to make it possible for miners in the US to walk off their jobs in support of strikers in Britain or Germany. So far, however, this has never been used in practice, and unions in other international industries such as steel, automobiles, textiles or electronics have yet to follow suit. They still remain intensely nationalistic in their outlooks.

As the capitalists become more and more openly parasitical, however, and participate less and less directly in the actual process of production and distribution, the working class grows to realize that it is capable of performing all of these tasks for itself, and that there is no longer any practical need for the individual capitalist. There is no function which the capitalist or their hired managers perform that the workers cannot themselves take over and do just as well.

Thus, as the economic crises and contradictions of capitalism increase, the working class begins to assume more and more control over the process of production and distribution. When the class struggle reaches the breaking point, the workers realize that they no longer need the capitalists, and are capable of seizing the productive forces which have been built by capitalism and running these productive forces themselves, for the mutual benefit of all.

This process, however, is not automatic or self-fulfilling. Socialism will not spring, fully-formed, from the forehead of Zeus. It must be actively organized for and fought for. It must be consciously made by an act of will on the part of the working class, which carries out the actions demanded by existing circumstances. In short, it must be made by a working class revolution.

FIVE:
Hegemony and Counter-Hegemony

So far in our analysis of capitalist social relationships, we have considered only the economic sphere of capitalist society. In order to understand the process of social development and change, however, we must also understand how the economic sphere is related to the rest of the social structure, and how capitalist economic relationships affect and are affected by such non-economic spheres as the family, the state, law, art and ethics.

As we have seen, the Marxian conception of history is based on the dialectical interpenetration of human social constructions with their natural surroundings. Human beings, according to this conception, must organize into certain social relationships in order to extract their necessaries of life from their surroundings. In doing so, however, human social structures have a profound impact on those surroundings. When the actions of human social practice alter this relationship beyond a certain point, the existing pattern of social organization is no longer suitable for dealing with these circumstances, and new social relationships become necessary. In this manner, Marx asserted, the dialectical interpenetration of humans with their surroundings produces the series of social changes we know of as history.

In a social system such as capitalism, which tends to view natural surroundings as an entity to be conquered and utilized for the production of profit, and which views economic activities as being governed by impersonal natural laws, a relational and interconnecting view of totality, such as Marxian dialectics, is difficult to grasp and understand. It is not surprising, then, that after Marx's death his outlook was simplified and modified by those who claimed to be his followers.

By the time of the Second International, Marxism had been, in practice, reduced to the simple formula, "Material conditions determine consciousness." Human society, these "dialectical materialists" asserted, developed according to laws which were regular and predictable, and which could be studied with the precision of a natural science.

The pinnacle of this "positivist" view was articulated by the Leninists, who confidently asserted, (a) human society develops according to absolute and knowable laws, (b) dialectical materialism is the method for "objectively" studying and understanding these laws, and thus is capable of predicting the course of development of human history, and (c) the vanguard party of trained dialectical materialists is capable of foreseeing this future and thus should lead human society in accordance with this view.

Leninist theory is most often presented in the form of the "base-superstructure" framework. According to this view, the economic relationships of human society are the "base" upon which society is founded, and all other social relationships (sexual, familial, racial, national) are merely a "superstructure" which is built upon this economic base. Prevailing economic conditions, these "economic determinists" assert, directly determine the form of religious, familial, legal, ethical and other social relationships, and these non-economic structures can only be altered through changes in the underlying economic base. As Stalin put it, "Every base has a superstructure corresponding to it. . . If the base changes or is eliminated, then following this its superstructure changes or is eliminated; if a new base arises, then following this a superstructure arises corresponding to it."

The Leninist "base-superstructure" paradigm is, however, incomplete and cannot describe bourgeois society as a whole. It focuses narrowly on the effects of economic relationships upon humans without recognizing that human actions have a profound effect upon economic relationships. The dialectical materialists have merely modified the idealist or religious outlook they claim to be criticizing, and have subjected the world to the same sort of alienation they condemn in others. Instead of asserting that God or Reason moves human beings, the economic materialists assert that The Dialectic does. Like the religious idealists, the dialectical materialists have rejected the role of human action in history.

Contrary to the view of the positivists, the social conflict between the worker and the owner is not merely economic in nature. The worker does not simply haggle with the boss over pay, working hours and surplus value; workers also fight for such non-economic goals as more control over the workplace, more decision-making power, and more opportunity for self-expression and self-fulfillment through work. The narrow economic point of view also ignores the effects of such non-economic forms of oppression as racism, sexism, nationalism and authoritarianism. These relationships are dismissed by the Leninists as mere "side issues" which distract the workers from the "real fight"—the economic struggle between worker and owner.

The Leninists thus tend to view each succeeding social mode of production in solely economic terms—merely as methods whereby humans produce their physical needs. In reality, however, no human society can exist unless it reproduces, alongside its physical needs, the whole array of ideas, attitudes and social relationships which allow it to exist. All social modes of production must determine, not only how the physical necessities of life are produced and distributed (economics), but also how the different members of that society relate to each other (nationality, race, gender, sexuality, religion) and how these social structures are maintained, enforced and indoctrinated (law, education, the state).

Thus, a mode of production is not merely economic in nature. It must also include the various ways in which any human society interacts with itself and with its surroundings, and how it is able to maintain and reproduce the conditions for its existence.

Marx never made the mistake of asserting that economic relationships were the determining factor in capitalist society. Rather, he realized that it is not enough for the capitalist to have a social structure that allows profits to be maximized; the social system must also continually reproduce the conditions under which profits can be made at all. The economic and non-economic spheres, Marx pointed out, exist in a dialectical relationship, with each influencing and reproducing the other. "Productive forces and social relations," he wrote, "[are] different sides of the development of the social individual":

> In the actual world, civil law, morality, the family, civil society, the state, etc., remain in existence, only they have become moments—states of existence and being of man— which have no validity in isolation, but dissolve and engender one another.
>
> This conception of history depends on our ability to expound the real process of production, starting out from the material production of life itself, and to comprehend the form of intercourse connected with this and created by this mode of production (i.e., civil society in its various stages), as the basis of all history; and to show it in its action as state, to explain all the different theoretical products and forms of consciousness, religion, philosophy, ethics, etc., etc., and trace their origins and growth from that basis; by which means, of course, the whole thing can be depicted in its

totality (and therefore, too, the reciprocal action of these various sides on one another).

Although Marx never asserted that human social reality was based on narrow economic structures, he and Engels deserve much of the blame for fueling this interpretation. Rather than referring to his philosophical outlook as "naturalism", Marx continued to call himself a "materialist" in an effort to separate himself clearly from Hegelian idealism, and thus reinforced later deterministic interpretations of his viewpoint. Marx also continued to overemphasize the role of economic structures in all of his works, since he was responding to idealist German philosophers who tended to give economic relationships no role at all in human affairs.

Nevertheless, both Marx and Engels attacked those who reduced Marxism to simple economic determinism. Engels wrote, "According to the materialist conception of history, the determining moment in history is ultimately the production and reproduction of real life. More than this neither Marx nor I have ever asserted. If therefore somebody twists this into the statement that the economic moment is the only determining one, he transforms it into a meaningless, abstract and absurd phrase."

Marx never lost sight of the interpenetration and co-determination of the economic and non-economic spheres. Towards the end of his life, he intended to write a whole series of books detailing the structure of the total capitalist mode of production, and intended to examine the role of various non-economic relationships in the reproduction of capitalist society. "I shall therefore publish," Marx wrote, "the critique of law, ethics, politics, etc., in a series of distinct, independent pamphlets, and afterwards try in a special work to present them again as an interconnected whole, showing the interrelationships of the separate parts."

Unfortunately, Marx only lived long enough to begin the first of this projected series, *Capital*, which dealt exclusively with capitalist economics.

In order to understand capitalist society, then, we must understand it holistically, as a totality. We must examine the non-economic relationships through which capitalist society reproduces and propagates itself.

Radical critics of bourgeois society who examine it from different points of view have identified several relational structures which help to form and propagate that society. Radical feminists, for instance, view society in terms of gender roles, and see relationships between male and female as the determining factor in social development. Anarchists examine society's structures of power and authority, and view the relationships between bosses and subordinates as the determining factor. Latino, African-American, Native American and other racial or national activists, by studying the relationships between races or nations, see racism and nationalism as the determining factors. Socialists and communists, of course, focus on class relationships, and see the social dynamic between workers and owners as the key to social development.

When we examine bourgeois society as a whole, however, we realize that each of these particular outlooks — feminism, anarchism, anti-racism, or socialism — is, by itself, incomplete. Each outlook reduces the whole of a society to a particular "base" of social relationships, with all other relationships subordinate to this base. This, however, is an abstraction that does not occur in reality. In a real living human society, all of these social relationships interpenetrate to mutually support and determine each other. None of them is any more "basic" or "fundamental" than the others. Bourgeois society does not exist merely to extract surplus value, nor to dominate women, nor to keep racial or ethnic groups in a disadvantaged position, nor to safeguard authority relationships, nor to build national power. Instead, bourgeois society exists as it does in order to do *all* of these things, and all of these things mutually interpenetrate to form bourgeois society as a whole, by reproducing the conditions which allow that society to reproduce itself.

In every sphere of bourgeois society, these co-determining social relationships can be found. In the workplace, workers and owners fight an economic battle over wages and profits, and the dynamics of this struggle are important to the economic structure of society. At the same time, the boss exercises authority over those subordinate to him, and the conflict between order-giver and order-taker is a function of the authority structures of bourgeois society. The dynamics between men and women in the workplace depend on society's gender roles, while the relationship between whites and people of color is a function of racial structures and roles.

In the bourgeois family, the same relationships are present. Most members of the family are dependent on the monetary income received by the family "breadwinner", and this relationship is a function of the economic structure. Some in the family unit exercise domination and authority over the others, according to the power relationships of society. Males and females carry out distinct roles within the family that are influenced by the gender roles of society as a whole. Finally, the relationship between different families is a function of race and nation.

In capitalist society, each sphere demonstrates the interdependence of these relationships. In the factory, the authority structures necessary for profit-making are based on modified family roles, with the boss as "father figure" and the workers as "children" and "siblings". In the family, gender roles are determined by the authority that comes from the economic position of breadwinner. In educational institutions, women and people of color receive training for roles which are "appropriate" for them, while the children of wealthy capital-owners receive training for positions of authority and leadership.

It is important to realize that none of these social relationships can exist without the others, since they are all inherent in human society itself. One cannot have gender relationships unless one first has human beings, but one cannot have human beings without first having economics to provide them with the necessaries of life. The same is true for racial, authority or national relationships.

At the same time, however, an economic system cannot exist unless society has determined what needs to be produced and for whom, and this is a function of that society's sexual, authority, racial and national roles. One cannot consider any of these social relationships in isolation, since each can only be defined in terms of the others. They are all fundamental, and form one dynamic whole.

Contrary to the assertions of the Leninists and the economic determinists, class-based economic relationships are not the "primary" cause of social development, with the others merely "secondary" to it. Rather, the close examination of any particular social relationship will show that *all* of these various factors are operating and that they reinforce and strengthen each other. An examination of economic roles shows that capitalists use racial and gender roles to keep workers divided and help to increase surplus value. At the same time, however, an examination of gender roles shows that men use economic inequalities to keep women financially dependent and thus in an inferior social position. By examining authority relationships, one can see that bosses use racial, gender and economic divisions to keep their subordinates in line and thus to preserve existing power structures.

In order to assert a nation's superiority in the world, that nation must keep other nations economically inferior by controlling their resources and cutting into their foreign trade. In this case, economic relationships are made to serve nationalist ends. On the other hand, in order to increase a nation's economic position over others, one must place other nations in an inferior position through military or political domination. In this instance, nationalist relationships are made to serve economic ends. In actual societies, neither point of view is dominant; rather, they both reinforce and perpetuate each other.

The source of the bourgeois class's power is not simply that it controls capital and thus places workers in a disadvantaged economic position. The ruling class's power comes from the fact that it is able to implement and reproduce a set of interconnecting social relationships which safeguard its position of privilege, and that it is able to defend these social relationships from the attempts of the oppressed to change them.

The primary sanction for people to stay within the assigned roles is negative reinforcement; by refusing to stay within "accepted" social roles, people cut themselves off from the various social relationships which surround them. For instance, a worker is not forced to work at wage labor and produce surplus value, but if she doesn't she gets no pay and cannot buy the necessities of life. A person who refuses to accept the established norms for family roles will not be able to marry and have a family, leading to social ostracism and financial hardship.

By using such reinforcement to threaten people into conforming to the accepted roles, bourgeois society is able to compel people to fit themselves into the established roles without the need for violence or coercion. Instead of fitting social roles around the individual, bourgeois society succeeds in compelling people to fit *themselves* into the accepted roles, and thus to modify their behavior in ways that serve to protect and propagate the social relationships which allow the bourgeois class to maintain its position of social privilege.

However, since the social relationships in bourgeois society are geared towards serving the needs of the ruling elite rather than social needs, fitting oneself into the accepted roles may mean that some of the individual's own social needs must go unfulfilled. If a woman is to obtain economic security within bourgeois society, for instance, she must conform to the expected roles of marriage and subservience to her husband. This, at the same time, precludes any possibility of forming a free and equal relationship between the genders. In order to maintain a relationship with his family and avoid ostracism, a gay man may have to stay closeted, thus making a free and open sexuality impossible. If a worker is to labor at a wage job to obtain the necessaries of life, he must accept the authority of the boss, and thus cannot seek self-fulfillment or creativity on the job.

Thus, even if capitalism were able to fulfill all of the material economic needs of its members, it is incapable of fulfilling all of their *non-economic* needs. Any unmet needs which are produced by bourgeois society, whether the need for shared decision-making, free and equal sexual roles, or for national self-determination, can become a potential source of discontent and challenge. And, since all of these social relationships interpenetrate and prop each other up, a challenge to any one has the potential to become a challenge to them all.

This possibility is combated by the social structures of bourgeois society, in which the various social relationships are set up precisely to safeguard the position of the ruling elite. In the same manner that capitalist economists justify capitalism as a system of eternal natural laws which operate independently of human will, bourgeois familial, racial, sexual, authority and national relationships are depicted as natural "givens" rather than as human social creations. In effect, bourgeois society uses social institutions as an alienating abstraction, hiding the human relationships which underlie these institutions and preventing the victims of these institutions from seeing that they can be altered in accordance with human desires. These alienating institutions are protected by their interconnections and by the negative social consequences of rejecting them.

Bourgeois society's inability to meet human needs, however, constantly produces people who reject its social roles, and whenever this alienation is overcome and social relationships are seen to be human creations rather than unchanging conditions of life, a radical consciousness results. Instead of merely reinterpreting these social relationships, the radical realizes that human actions can *change* them, in accordance with human needs and desires.

Furthermore, radical consciousness which results in a desire to change one set of social institutions brings with it the possibility of changing the totality of human social institutions, of substituting a new social structure for the existing one. In other words, it brings the possibility of a *revolutionary* consciousness.

This process is aided by the interpenetration of bourgeois social relationships. Once one realizes that sexual roles are artificial and serve to benefit males, it is not a large step to realize that white wealthy men in positions of authority benefit more from sexism than do poor men of color who have no power, and thus racism, authority and economic roles are also a factor in the oppression of women. In the same way, anarchists see that power relationships bring the most benefit to white wealthy males, and that sexual, class and racial roles play a part in determining authority relationships. Communists see that capital-owners tend to be white men in positions of authority, and that class relations are influenced by race, gender and authority relations. In essence, each of these radical critiques of bourgeois society comes to see that it is fighting the same narrow ruling elite as the others, and that each of these movements is fighting the same socio-political ruling elite on a different front.

The Leninist economic determinists are clearly wrong when they assert that all revolutionary consciousness has its roots in economic relationships. In many instances, revolutionary awareness has come from an explicitly non-economic relationship. In anti-colonial rebellions such as those in Algeria or Ireland, it is racial and national relationships which provoke the outbreak, not merely economic exploitation.

In South Africa, racial relationships were obviously much more important than economic ones in sparking anti-apartheid rebellion. The US civil rights movement was not an economic struggle—no capitalist would lose money by allowing African-Americans to drink at the same water fountain or ride in the front of a bus—yet this movement was bitterly resisted by bourgeois society. The capitalists realized that these non-economic challenges represented a direct threat to bourgeois norms of race and authority, and so represented a potential revolutionary challenge to the system as a whole.

The realization that revolutionary consciousness can come from a number of social relationships and conflicts, opens bourgeois society to attack on several fronts. Rather than being mere "side issues" which "divide the working class", the struggle over non-economic relationships performs a vital task in undermining the various structures of bourgeois society and producing a revolutionary consciousness.

If the hegemony of the bourgeois social system is to be broken, then, it must be attacked and combated on each front, and these various struggles must reinforce and complement each other. In essence, revolutionaries must undermine *all* existing social relationships which benefit the ruling elite and put new social relationships in their place—the bourgeois cultural hegemony must be replaced by a new hegemony.

And, since the social relationships of this new hegemony must be determined by social needs and desires, any anti-bourgeois revolution must place, not merely the economic means of production, but the entire mode of life, including familial, sexual, racial, gender, national and authority roles, under social control. Rather than serving the needs of the ruling elite, these relationships must serve the needs of the social whole. The revolution must be truly *social*-ist.

SIX:
Critique of Leninism

The theme of hegemony and counter-hegemony arose as part of a larger attack on the Leninist paradigm by the growing council communist movement. The council movement, led by Anton Pannekoek, Hermann Gorter, Karl Korsch and Antonio Gramsci, launched a comprehensive attack on every facet of Leninism, from its philosophical assumptions to its practical programs for socialist revolution.

The philosophical basis of Leninism had been laid out in 1908 in Lenin's work *Materialism and Empirio-Criticism*. In this work, the subtle distinctions of Marx's dialectical view of totality were lost. Rather than the Marxian interpenetration between mind and matter—"Thinking and being are certainly distinct, but are at the same time in unity with each other"— Lenin took the view that all outlooks and philosophies are either idealist or materialist, with nothing in between. Lenin dismisses as "litter and rubbish" any attempts to form a unity between these two philosophical frameworks: "The attempt to escape these two basic trends in philosophy is nothing but 'conciliatory quackery'."

Marxism, Lenin repeatedly asserted, was a materialist outlook—material (economic) factors were the sole determinant of human actions. In an argument which broke out among socialists over the outlooks of the physicist Ernst Mach, Lenin asserted that material reality is objectively independent of human thought, that the "real world" exists "out there" and operates without regard to the position or viewpoint of the observer. Human thoughts themselves, Lenin asserted, were material things, since they were the result of the motion of molecules and chemicals in the human brain.

Since material reality was independent of consciousness, Lenin concluded, there exists some "objective truth" which corresponds to existing material reality. The process of human knowledge, as the Leninists came to see it, is "reflective"; ideas are merely the mental reflections of an objective material reality, and those ideas that could be shown through practice to correspond to material reality were objectively "true".

It is easy to see how Lenin's political outlooks developed from this philosophical base. If the world operates independently of humans according to objective laws, then it is possible for humans to discover those laws, and thus come to a "scientific understanding" of the operation of human society. The Marxist-Leninist party, being trained in the methods of "dialectical materialism", could understand these laws and interpret them to those who were less "conscious". Therefore, the task of interpreting the laws of history for the working class fell to the trained cadre of Leninists who would rule in their name.

The most in-depth criticism of Lenin's crude materialism was made by the Dutch council communist Anton Pannekoek. Pannekoek, a professional astronomer, drew on the newly-developed frameworks of quantum mechanics and Einsteinian relativity to attack Lenin's notion of "objective reality". The properties of matter, Pannekoek pointed out, were merely abstractions which depended upon the point of view of the observer.

Light, for instance, can be viewed as a wave of electromagnetic energy or as a particle of concentrated matter. One group of nuclear physicists had demonstrated the "photovoltaic effect", in which beams of light could be observed to knock out electrons from sheets of metal. This experiment indicated that light was made up of tiny particles.

Other groups of physicists, however, used the "double-slit" experiment to demonstrate that beams of light produced the same interference patterns typical of waves. This result seemed to indicate that light was made up of electromagnetic waves. Even more startling, beams of nuclear particles such as protons or electrons also exhibited wave interference patterns when they were shot through a double slit, indicating that they, too, are made up of waves.

Both viewpoints could not be "objectively" true. Matter could not be at the same time a particle, which is concentrated within a limited area, and a wave, which spreads out over a large area. The properties of matter seem to depend on the point of view of the observer; if you look for particles, you will see particles, and if you look for waves, you will see waves. In fact, quantum mechanics demonstrates, matter is neither a particle nor a wave until some observer makes that determination. Matter has no "objective reality" — what it is depends upon who is making the observation.

Since the structure of objective reality depends in large part on the viewpoint of the observer, Pannekoek concluded, Lenin's definition of materialism as "the primacy of matter" was much too narrow. "If . . . matter is taken as the name for the philosophical concept denoting objective reality," says Pannekoek, "it embraces far more than physical matter." It also must include the thoughts and conceptions of the person who is doing the observing. Matter influences the structure of idea,

Pannekoek concluded, but at the same time the structure of matter was influenced by conceptions and ideas. Thus Pannekoek rejected the crude materialism of Lenin and returned to the dialectical naturalism originally proposed by Marx.

The debate over Lenin's "objective reality" was more than an abstract intellectual debate—it had profound practical implications. Lenin, by arguing that reality existed independently of human consciousness, was led to embrace the strategy of "injecting" a radical consciousness into the working class, in accordance with the "laws" of economic determinism and dialectical materialism.

The council communists, however, rejected Lenin's materialism and argued that subjectivity and objectivity were interrelated. Objective conditions alone could not bring about social change; social change required social action. In contrast to the "scientific Marxists", who treated socialism as an historical inevitability, the council communists saw that socialist revolution would require a conscious act of will on the part of the working class, and a self-developed instrument of organization to bring this revolution about. The social organization adopted by the council communists was the worker's council.

The framework of the worker's council was born in the turbulent upheavals in Europe between 1917 and 1920. In the wake of the Russian revolution in February 1917, a wave of radicalism swept over Europe. In Italy, the industrial workers of Turin and Genoa seized a number of factories and paralyzed the authorities with a general strike In Germany, the government tottered on the brink of collapse, as strikes and worker uprisings came within a hair's breadth of seizing power. In Hungary, the government actually fell, and a "Soviet Government" held power for a short time. In all of these militant movements, the instrument of organization was the worker's council, an elected body of workers from each plant who organized and carried out the rebellions.

The new form of organization was seized on by militant revolutionaries as an alternative to the reformist Social Democratic parties. The Social Democrats advocated capturing the existing state through election campaigns and then legislating for government ownership of industries—their definition of "socialism". This strategy was attacked by the new council communists. "'Statifying' companies," declared Anton Pannekoek, "is not socialism; socialism is the power of the proletariat." The Italian communist Antonio Gramsci wrote that the future instruments of worker control could be seen in the worker's councils:

> The socialist state already exists potentially in the institutions of social life characteristic of the exploited working class. To link these institutions, co-ordinating and ordering them into a highly centralized hierarchy of competence and powers, while respecting the necessary autonomy and articulation of each, is to create a genuine worker's democracy here and now—a worker's democracy in effective and active opposition to the bourgeois state, and prepared to replace it here and now in all its essential functions of administering and controlling the national heritage.

During the "Two Red Years" of 1919-1920, Gramsci encouraged workers in the industrial plants to transform their "workshop committees" into worker's councils that would be capable of taking over and running the plant directly and democratically.

In 1917, the Russians had deposed the Tsar and the Provisional Government by organizing into *soviets* (from the Russian word for "council"). The European council communists praised the Soviet form of government, believing it to be based on the direct democratic control of the workplace by worker's councils. The Dutch communist Hermann Gorter pronounced, "This supple and flexible organism is the world's first socialist regime."

When word began to filter back about the Bolshevik brand of "democratic centralism", however, the council movement changed its stance toward the Russian Revolution. In 1920, when Otto Rühle toured the Soviet Union as a delegate to the Second Congress of the Communist International, he reported that the Soviets were mere tools of the ruling Bolshevik Party, and were "not councils in a revolutionary sense". Instead, he concluded, the Leninists were ruling through "bureaucracy, the deadly enemy of the council system".

A steady stream of criticism began. Pannekoek wrote, "If the most important element of the revolution consists in the masses taking their own affairs—the management of society and production—in hand themselves, then any form of organization which does not permit control and direction by the masses themselves is counter-revolutionary and harmful."

When the Bolsheviks, through the Third International, began to mold the other Communist Parties to their own image, the council movement responded with calls for democracy and rank-and-file control. Gramsci, from his prison cell in Italy, criticized the Italian Communists, calling for "a greater intervention of the proletarian elements in the life of the party and a diminution of the powers of the bureaucracy":

> The error of the party has been to have accorded priority in an abstract fashion to the problem of party organization, which in practice has simply meant creating an apparatus of party functionaries who could be depended upon for their orthodoxy towards the official view. It was believed, and is still believed, that the revolution depends only on the existence of such an apparatus; and it is sometimes even believed that its existence can bring about the revolution.

Hermann Gorter bluntly declared, "The Russian tactics of dictatorship by party and leadership cannot possibly be correct here." Pannekoek attacked the elitist outlooks of the Leninists. "What can a small party, however principled, do when what is needed are the masses?" he asked. "And it also follows from this theory that it is not even the entire communist party that exercises dictatorship, but the Central Committee, and this it does first within the Party itself, where it takes it upon itself to expel individuals and uses shabby means to get rid of opposition." Lenin responded with a work entitled *Left-Wing Communism; An Infantile Disorder*, which attacked the council movement as "anarchist" and "undisciplined".

As the Communist Party entrenched itself more and more firmly in the Soviet Union, the attacks of the council communists became more vehement. In April 1920, Pannekoek announced, "The Executive Committee in Moscow and the leading comrades in Russia have come down completely on the side of opportunism." Pannekoek charged the Soviet Union with using the international communist movement as a tool of its own nationalistic programs:

> The Third International, as the association of communist parties preparing proletarian revolution in every country, is not formally bound by the policies of the Russian government, and it is supposed to pursue its own tasks completely independent of the latter. In practice, however, this separation does not exist; just as the Communist Party is the backbone of the Soviet Republic, the executive committee is intimately connected with the Presidium of the Soviet Republic through the persons of its members, thus forming an instrument whereby the Presidium intervenes in the politics of Western Europe. We can now see why the tactics of the Third International, laid down by congress to apply homogeneously to all capitalist countries and to be directed from the center, are determined not only by the needs of communist agitation in those countries, but also by the political needs of Soviet Russia.

Pannekoek's fears were confirmed after the rise of Stalin and the subsequent flip-flops of the Comintern program. Before the outbreak of World War II, after Stalin signed a non-aggression Pact with Hitler, the Communist Parties were instructed to intensify the fight against the Social Democratic parties in Europe, who were to be considered as being objectively no different from the fascists—"social-fascists". As soon as Hitler invaded Russia, however, this tune abruptly changed: now the Communist Parties were instructed to form coalitions with the Social Democrats as part of a "united front of anti-fascist forces". "The politics of Lenin," Pannekoek concluded, "had their logical culmination in Stalinism in Russia."

Karl Korsch also fought against the domination of the Comintern by the USSR, remarking in disgust that the international movement had been reduced to "the one 'Marxist-Leninist' doctrine which alone brings salvation." Gorter wrote, "If the Russian tactics are still pursued here after all the disastrous consequences that they have already had here, then it will no longer be stupidity, but a crime; a crime against the revolution."

In 1921, when the sailors at the Kronstadt Fortress mutinied in an attempt to overthrow the Communist Party and re-institute the Soviet government and direct worker control, the council communists cheered them on. "Now that the proletariat in Kronstadt has risen up against you, the communist party," Gorter wrote, "now that you have had to declare a state of emergency in Petrograd against the proletariat . . . has the thought still not occurred to you, even now, that dictatorship by the proletariat is really preferable to dictatorship by the party?" Gorter concluded:

> Your real fault, which neither we nor history can forgive, is to have foisted a counter-revolutionary program and tactics upon the world proletariat, and to have rejected the really revolutionary ones which could have saved us.

The protests of the council movement were in vain, however. The Bolsheviks succeeded in imposing a program of "21 Points" upon the Comintern parties that effectively made them instruments of Stalin's Central Committee. The "left-wing" council communists were expelled from the party, and most went into exile and obscurity. The ruling Bolsheviks removed the last vestiges of the Soviet government, crushed rank-and-file rebellions led by the Kronstadt sailors and by the Ukrainian councilist Nestor Makhno, and expelled and purged the councilist "Worker Opposition" within the Soviet government. In essence, the Bolsheviks installed "socialism" by destroying socialism. By 1925, the council communist movement had all but ceased to exist.

By 1991, however, the council communists had been vindicated — Leninism had proven itself to be bankrupt and discredited. Leninist regimes in the USSR and Eastern Europe had collapsed, and those in China, Cuba and North Korea seemed to be on the verge of doing the same.

Despite the collapse of these Leninist regimes, however, a number of Marxist organizations continue to preach the organizational and revolutionary principles adopted by Lenin or by one of his disciples — Trotsky, Mao or Castro. In formulating a model for socialist revolution in the industrialized countries, then, we must first examine this existing model and learn what we can from it.

In this chapter, we will examine the programs of twoof the largest and most active of the North American revolutionary groups, the Revolutionary Communist Party (RCP) and the Progressive Labor Party (PLP). Both of these parties claim allegiance to the Maoist variation of Leninism.

Like all Leninists, the RCP and PLP conclude that workers are always reformist and will never develop a revolutionary consciousness on their own, and that such a consciousness must be brought to them by the dedicated vanguard party. The Progressive Labor Party says: "Throughout the process of seizing, holding and expanding revolutionary power, workers will need only one political force — the communist party." The Revolutionary Communist Party echoes this outlook, saying, "The proletariat in this country has among its ranks and at the head of its class-conscious section its own revolutionary political party, the Revolutionary Communist Party USA, which is armed with the revolutionary outlook of the international proletariat, Marxism-Leninism, Mao Tse-Tung Thought."

The idea of the vanguard revolutionary party that would educate and organize the working class in revolutionary principles was original to Lenin, who wrote in his pamphlet *What is to be Done?*:

> I assert; (1) that no movement can be made durable without a stable organization of leaders to maintain continuity; (2) that the more widely the masses are drawn into the struggle and form the basis of the movement, the more it is necessary to have such all organization and the more stable it must be; (3) that the organization must consist chiefly of persons engaged in revolution as a profession; (4) that, in a country with a despotic government, the more we restrict membership of this organization, the more difficult it will be to catch this organization; and (5) the wider will be the circle of men and women of the working class or other classes of society to perform active work in it.

Following the Leninist line, Mao Zedong would later write:

> If there is to be a revolution, there must be a revolutionary party. Without a revolutionary party, without a party built on the Marxist-Leninist revolutionary style, it is impossible to lead the working class and the broad masses of the people in defeating imperialism and its running dogs.

Marx, however, asserted that socialist revolution developed from changes in social conditions brought about by the dialectical interpenetration of humans and their surroundings. As Marx writes:

> These conditions of life, which different generations find in existence, decide also whether or not the periodically occurring revolutionary convolutions will be strong enough to overthrow the basis of the entire existing system. And if those material elements of a complete revolution are not present, (namely, on the one hand the existing productive forces, on the other the formation of a revolutionary mass, which revolts against not only the separate conditions of society up till then, but against the very "production of life" till then, the "total activity" on which it is based), then as far as practical development is concerned, it is absolutely immaterial whether the idea of the revolution has been expressed a hundred times already, as the history of communism proves.

> In order to abolish the idea of private property, the idea
> of communism is quite sufficient. It takes actual communist
> action to abolish actual private property.

Marx pointed out that any attempt to socialize the productive forces of society before they were developed enough to provide abundance to a communal economy would be to simply "socialize poverty", and thus to "start the old shit all over again."

Marx also concluded that socialism could result only from the direct action of the working class, which would be forced to organize itself into a revolutionary body in response to the intolerable conditions of late monopoly capitalism. Revolution, Marx wrote, could only come about through a militant working class organization: "It can be affected through a union, which by the character of the proletariat itself can only be a universal one."

Thus, Marx concluded, the working class would organize itself in response to changing conditions; there was no need for an outside revolutionary clique to "inject" a revolutionary consciousness or to "make" the revolution, since the deteriorating social conditions would have already made it to a large extent. All that remained was for a working class organization to sweep aside the old order and replace it. "Force," wrote Marx, "is the midwife of every old society that is pregnant with a new."

The revolutionary party, Marx writes, would not be a force separate from the working class, but instead would be an integral part of it:

> In what relation do the Communists stand to the
> proletarians as a whole? The Communists do not form a
> separate party opposed to other working class parties. They
> have no interests separate and apart from those of the
> proletariat as a whole. They do not set up any sectarian
> principles of their own by which to shape and mold the
> proletarian movement.

Marx thus rejected the notion of a centralized party of professional revolutionaries which directed the revolution while educating the workers to communist principles. The Leninists fail to see that the revolution does not develop from the party; rather, the party develops from the need for revolution.

The Leninists, however, continue to call for a "revolutionary dictatorship". The PLP "says explicitly that the leadership, the party, wants to encourage direct working class transformation of society, but that, when push comes to shove, in an ultimate sense, the power of the society should rest in the hands of the party, rather than in the hands of some non-party group, or some sort of coalition between the party and non-Communist forces."

The Leninists assert that their "dictatorship of the proletariat" means that the party will "represent" the working class while in power. The only way, however, that the revolutionary party can truly represent the working class is if the party *is* the working class — the working class organized as a whole. Any other party would be, not a party *of* the working class, but a party *in behalf of* the working class.

This is all very well, so long as the interests of the party are the same as the interests of the working class. However, as the history of Leninism proves, the interests of the "vanguard party" cannot be those of the working class. Inevitably, the party turns into a party *over* the working class.

The PLP and RCP, like their counterparts in China and the USSR, openly declare that they intend to place their party in exclusive power after the revolution. The PLP says:

> After the revolution, workers and their allies will not need a government separate from the party. Either such a government would be a rubber-stamp for the workers' mass party, or it would represent an enemy of communism. Surely a rubber-stamp government is useless and deceptive, and workers must never again share power with class enemies. We propose that, after the revolution, the party — composed of millions of workers — lead society.

The RCP echoes:

> The basic first step of the proletariat, having won political power, is to take into its hands, through its state and the leadership of its party, the decisive levers and lifelines of the economy. . . In short, it socializes ownership of the major means of production, and institutes basic overall planning of the economy in accordance with this, through the proletarian state.
>
> Between capitalist and communist society there lies a long transition period of socialism in which the proletariat . . . must maintain and strengthen its dictatorship and the socialization of the ownership of the means of production, strike at, restrict and move towards eliminating the differences and inequalities left over from the old society and transform the thinking of the people according to the scientific principles and outlooks of Marxism.

This of course, would quickly lead to a situation such as existed in the Soviet Union. Since only the party is wise enough to know what issues are worthy of public attention, the press would have to submit to its "guidance"; since only party members can decide what best serves the interests of the working class, officials and bureaucrats would have to submit to "party discipline". Above all, since only the party can master the subtleties of dialectical materialism and thus know what is in the "real" interests of the working class, it alone should be given the power to make political and economic decisions.

The only real way of approaching socialism, as Marx and the council communists repeatedly stressed, is through a free and democratic association of self-managing producers.

In 1871, the working class of Paris succeeded in creating a revolutionary government that held power for a short time before being brutally and bloodily suppressed. The Commune was an important event for Marx and Engels. Until 1871, Marx had assumed that the working class would be able to seize the existing institutions of the bourgeois republic and use them as the basis for a socialist government after the revolution.

The Commune, however, completely changed Marx's thinking on this point, and made such a profound impact on him that he added an amendment to the *Communist Manifesto* on the matter. The Commune was, he wrote, the "political form at last discovered under which to work out the economic emancipation of labor."

In concluding our analysis of the Leninist model of revolution, therefore, we will study the program of the Commune, in order to compare the Leninist state to a true revolutionary society, one that existed not merely in words and phrases, but within definite historical circumstances.

The first order of business for the Commune was the complete destruction of the old bourgeois state apparatus. Marx writes;

> From the outset, the Commune was compelled to recognize that the working class, once come to power, could not manage with the old state machine; that in order not to lose again its only just conquered supremacy, the working class must, on the one hand, do away with all the old repressive machinery, previously used against itself, and on the other hand, safeguard itself against its own deputies and officials by declaring them all, without exception, subject to recall at any moment.

Engels hailed this action by the Commune as a "shattering of the former state power and its replacement by a new and real democratic state."

Lenin, in his pre-October days, writes of the similarity of the structure of the Paris Commune with the fledgling Russian *soviets*, or councils. Indeed, in his remarkable booklet *State and Revolution*, Lenin envisions the *soviet* as serving at the center of a Russian socialist system in terms very similar to those pictured by the council communists and embodied in the Commune. During his discussion of the *soviets*, Lenin pointed out that the Parisian revolutionary government was fundamentally different from the bourgeois state which it attempted to replace;

> The Commune substitutes for the venal and rotten parliamentarianism of bourgeois society institutions in

which freedom of opinion and of discussion does not degenerate into deception, for the parliamentarians themselves have to work, have to execute their own laws, have themselves to test their results in real life, and to render account directly to their constituents. Representative institutions remain, but there is no parliamentarianism here as a special system, as the division of labor between the legislative and the executive as a privileged position for the representatives. We cannot imagine, democracy, even proletarian democracy, without representative institutions, but we can and must imagine democracy without parliamentarianism.

The Commune, Marx points out, operated on the principle of direct democracy:

> The Commune was formed of the municipal councilors, chosen by universal suffrage in the various wards of the town, responsible and revocable at short terms. The majority of its members were naturally working men, or acknowledged representatives of the working class. The Commune was to be a working, not a parliamentary body, executive and legislative at the same time. Instead of continuing to be the agents of the central government, the police were at once stripped of their political attributes, and turned into the responsible and at all times revocable agents of the Commune. So were officials of all other branches of the administration. From the members of the Commune downwards, the public service had to be done at workmen's wages. The vested interests and the representation allowances of the high dignitaries of state disappeared along with the high dignitaries themselves. . . The whole of the educational institutions were opened up to the public gratuitously, and at the same time cleared of all interference of church and state. . . Like the rest of public servants, magistrates and judges were to be elected, responsible and revocable.

The Commune was composed largely of Blanquists and Proudhonists, but, as usual, practical necessities forced the Communards to abandon ideology in favor of practical measures. The resulting Commune was claimed by both Marxists and Bakuninists, but clearly it owed a great deal to both.

Marx noted that the state built by the Commune was no longer a "state" — that is, it was no longer the political instrument of a ruling class. The Commune was not a state that stood outside of society or over it; it was, rather, a government formed directly from the ordinary people and directly responsible to them.

Not all governmental functions disappeared under the Commune. There was still a need for such things as record-keeping and the enforcement of criminal laws. These functions were, however, stripped of their political and class functions. Marx writes:

> While the merely repressive organs of the old governmental power were to be amputated, its legitimate functions were to be wrested from an authority usurping pre-eminence over society itself, and restored to the responsible agents of society.

Thus, the necessary governmental functions were returned as fully as possible to freely elected officials under the direct control of their electors. In this way, the features of Leninist repression — the political police, the entrenched party bureaucrats, the farcical elections, the state apparatus of censorship and judicial repression, the lopsided distribution of wealth — were avoided.

The Commune recognized that even its meager state apparatus had the potential to become an entrenched elite, and introduced several measures to combat any tendency towards a self-perpetuating bureaucracy. Marx writes;

> Against the transformation of the state and the agents of the state from the servants of society into the masters of society — an inevitable transformation in all previous states — the Commune made use of two infallible expedients. In the first place, it filled all posts -- administrative, judicial and educational — by election on the basis of universal suffrage of all concerned, with the right of these same electors to recall their delegates at any time. And in the second place, all, officials, high or low, were paid only the wages received by other workers.

The Commune also recognized that a standing army that was responsible only to the government was merely a repressive tool. "The first decree of the Commune, therefore," writes Marx, "was the suppression of the standing army and the substitution for it of the armed people." The citizens of Paris were given basic military training and were organized into local militias to defend themselves from outside threats and internal counter-revolution. The best guarantee to keep a government responsible to the population, the Communards concluded, was to arm that population.

The Commune also recognized that the revolutionary government in Paris would not last if it could not encompass all of the country. While it lacked the means to carry out a national revolution, and thus fell to the guns of Versailles and Prussia, the Commune did lay a plan for a national revolutionary government under which to continue the social revolution. As Marx reports, "The cry of 'social republic' with which the Revolution of February was ushered in by the Paris proletariat, did but express a vague aspiration after a republic that was not only to supersede the monarchical form of class rule, but class rule itself. The Commune was the positive form of that republic":

> In a rough sketch of national organization which the Commune had no time to develop, it states clearly that the Commune was to be the political form of even the smallest country hamlet, and that in the rural districts the standing army was to be replaced with a national militia with an extremely short term of service. The rural communes of every district were to administer their common affairs by an assembly of delegates to the central town, and these district assemblies were again to send delegates to the National Delegation in Paris, each delegate bound by the mandat imperatif of his constituents.

The local Communes were to be autonomous and elected, but they were not intended to be independent political entities. "The Communal Constitution," Marx wrote, "has been mistaken for an attempt to break up the nation into a federation of small states. The antagonism of the Commune against the state power has been mistaken for an exaggerated form of the ancient struggle against over-centralization." Instead, the Commune was to provide a national organization with the greatest possible local autonomy, while still maintaining a national framework.

Some tasks, such as the coordination of the national economy and the mobilization for national defense, had to be coordinated by a central government at the national level. The Commune's plans, however, recognized that this body had to be monitored and regulated. "The few but important tasks which still would remain for a central government were not to be suppressed," Marx writes, "but were to be discharged by Communal and therefore, strictly responsible agents."

In short, Marx concluded, the Commune proved that the old bourgeois form of government would "have to give way to the self-government of the producers."

It is this idea of "self-government of the producers" that separates the program of Marx and the council communists from the Leninists. Leninism in all its forms flatly rejects the notion of worker self-government. The Leninists fight, not for a government made up of the organized proletariat, but for an authoritarian party bureaucracy that acts "in the interests of the proletariat".

The Commune's program, by contrast, would have produced a national revolutionary government made up of autonomous decentralized self-governing bodies, a free association of producers such as that envisioned by the syndicalists. Such a system can only be brought about by a broad mass-based movement which organizes the working class as a whole into a self-governing body.

The Paris Commune, we can see, was the first tentative step towards communist democracy. It was in essence a classless society; a government with no oppressed class to hold in check and no interests of its own to safeguard. It was not a government over the workers, but a government of the workers, whose sole task was to administrate and coordinate the activity of the self-governing producers.

The Commune stands in sharp contrast to the repressive states of the Leninist tradition. The Communist state, with its massive parasitic bureaucracy, falls far short of the Commune's popularly-elected, revocable and responsible agents. Rather than "withering away", the Leninist states grew ever larger and more parasitic until they finally could be tolerated no longer. The Leninist monstrosities have nothing in common with the communist democracy foreseen by Marx and the council communists and practiced at the Commune.

Serious socialist revolutionaries must, therefore, reject the Leninist model as being unsuited to the social and theoretical circumstances existing in the industrialized nations. It is clear that our revolutionary organizations and methods must be broad-based, mass-supported and based on the decentralized association of producers. This is the essence of the Worker's Council.

SEVEN:
The Worker's Council

The program of the worker's council movement finds its theoretical source in Marx's conclusion that the emancipation of the working class must be the work of the working class itself. No outside force is capable of organizing the working class and leading it to victory—that is a path that workers must trod by themselves.

The worker's council movement must therefore reject the Leninist notion of a vanguard party of professional revolutionaries. Such a program is based on a fundamental mistrust of the working class. Rather than a party which directs the struggle on behalf of the masses, council communists view the party as being a mass organization made up of the working class as a whole. The role of this revolutionary apparatus is merely to serve as a coordinator and clearinghouse for the working class as a whole. Council communists therefore have no party program which workers must adhere to, and no central authority that decides on matters of orthodoxy. Orthodoxy is a matter for the Church, not for a revolutionary organization.

The council communist movement also must reject the revisionist "Social Democrat" strategy of using politics and election coalitions to "capture the state" and thus legislate socialism into existence. Any legal political party which seeks to use elections and the electoral process to bring about change, must of necessity use "legal" methods, and must of necessity confine its actions to those which will not place it outside of the legal framework within which it wishes to operate. However, to be a real radical "alternative", the party must pursue goals and aims which fall outside the traditional framework and outside the existing system, and which are therefore by definition "illegal". It is impossible to utilize a political system for instituting changes which fall outside the accepted parameters of that system.

Any proposal which the bourgeois parties will accept or give support to must of necessity be acceptable to the capitalist order, and therefore is *a priori* nonrevolutionary. The whole process of compromising with bourgeois parties in legislative voting blocs and electoral alliances means that no measures will ever be adopted which are unacceptable to the bourgeois parties and the capitalist order. The party degenerates into a hollow shell which, while mouthing revolutionary platitudes, does nothing more than any other liberal bourgeois reform party would do. The party becomes revolutionary in name only.

All of these reformist parties seek legislation to insure that labor power is sold at more favorable terms, to make wage labor more palatable for the worker. None of these organizations upholds the revolutionary goal of abolishing the wage system, of ending the sale of labor power as a commodity.

The wage relationship is the linchpin of the entire capitalist system — the capitalist cannot extract a dime of profit if he is unable to purchase the labor power of those who have no capital. To be a socialist is to fight for the abolition of the wage system — anything less is not socialism, but liberal reformism. By refusing to call for the abolition of the wage system, the

Social Democrats and most of the parliamentary "Communist Parties" have lost all claim to the title "radical".

The only way for the socialist movement to prevent this is to build up an alternative political and social structure which is *independent* of the parliamentary party. The seizure of power by the working class, therefore, must consist not of strengthening the parliamentary party so it can seize the bourgeois state, but of strengthening the worker's councils so they can become a *new* governmental structure, a proletarian power base which destroys and replaces the entire bourgeois political apparatus. Socialists seek to capture the capitalist state, not so that they can utilize it for their own ends, but so they can destroy it to make room for their own power structures.

Therefore, any real radical working class movement must seek, not to use the present system to institute social changes, but to create and expand a completely new system, a new political structure which reflects the new social relationships. We cannot build an alternative to capitalism unless we can build an alternative *outside of* capitalism, in institutions and relationships which exist alongside present institutions but which are in opposition to them, which are in the system but not of it. These institutions are the worker's councils.

Other theorists have recognized the need for an authentically working-class form of organization, and have emphasized the need for independent worker's councils. Georgi Lukacs and Antonio Gramsci wrote of the councils, and the council communists Anton Pannekoek and Karl Korsch made them the centerpiece of their revolutionary strategy. Even Lenin, in his *State and Revolution*, follows the position of the council communists on most substantive matters. Lenin later, however, ignored much of what he had written.

In every instance where the workers have been forced to safeguard their own interests, they have responded by forming worker's councils. The French, in 1848 and 1871, turned to the commune, a local worker's self-government which functioned in every way as an authentic worker's council. The Russian working class, in 1905 and 1917, turned to the *soviets* (from the Russian word for "council"). Until the *soviets* came to be dominated by the Leninists, they stood as examples of worker self-government.

During the Russian Civil War, the syndicalist Nestor Makhno set up councils all over the Ukraine before he was crushed by Trotsky and his Red Army. In Germany and Hungary in the post-World War period, workers formed local councils during militant uprisings, as did the Hungarian revolutionaries in 1956. The Italian working class, during the strike of 1919-1920, formed local councils, as did the workers in Turin and other industrial centers during the militant class struggles of the 1970's. During the Spanish Civil War, large tracts of Republican territory were run by elected local councils. And the Polish revolutionaries of 1989 coordinated their struggle with local worker's councils.

Thus, the council movement is a trend within the socialist movement that seeks to organize the workers at the very point in which they are exploited — in the workplace. Rather than depending on the bourgeois election process or on simple trade union activity, the council communist movement asserts that the power of the capitalists can only be effectively fought by direct action at its source — in the process of production.

In its earliest form, the worker's council develops from the exploitative and undemocratic conditions found in the capitalist workplace. The bourgeois parliamentary republic gives the illusion that there is political democracy, that is, that the people who make the decisions which affect our lives are the elected and responsible representatives of their constituents. The basic human rights of free speech, free assembly, etc., are safeguarded by law.

In the economic sphere, however, there is not even the pretense of democracy; these constitutional guarantees simply do not apply to one-third of the worker's life. For eight hours a day, from the moment we cross the door to our place of work, we are subject to an authority which is arbitrary, unelected, unchecked and undemocratic.

The working class soon recognizes the conflict between the democracy and freedom that is promised and the harsh totalitarianism which is produced. Political officials in the bourgeois republic are said to be elected and responsible — they must justify their decisions and actions to their constituents. The owner of a business, however, is elected by no one and has not the slightest need to justify his actions to anybody, even when those actions have a direct and negative impact on our lives and communities.

If an elected official fails to justify his actions, or if he brings harm to the public interest, we can vote him out of office and replace him with someone who better represents us. If the business-owner takes actions which are harmful, we can do nothing. The worker's only "right" is to quit and work for another boss (who is equally free to treat his workers as he likes).

If we want to remove an elected official, we can freely criticize him and organize to remove him or check his power. In the capitalist workplace, however, there is absolutely no freedom of speech or assembly. Workers who dare to criticize the boss or the company can be fired on the spot.

In the bourgeois republic, we are supposedly protected against the arbitrary misuse of power by public officials. The owner of a business, however, is under no such restrictions. He may take disciplinary action against any worker for any reason. The boss may make and enforce arbitrary "rules" concerning everything from what his workers may wear on the job to when they can go to the bathroom. There is no right to a trial by a jury of one's peers, no right to face one's accuser, no right to protection from arbitrary punishment — in the capitalist workplace, none of these democratic rights exist.

In short, the workplace under capitalism does not resemble a democracy where people are protected against the misuse of power—rather, it resembles a totalitarian dictatorship where one person, the boss, wields unlimited power.

This does not mean, however, that the evils of capitalism are due solely to the evils of its individual business owners. It is not simply a matter of individual capitalists being greedy heartless people who don't care about their workers and are out to simply squeeze as much money from them as they can. Workers come to recognize that it is the *entire social system itself* which is its enemy, not merely the individual capitalists who make it up.

A business owner may be the sweetest person in the world; he may give money to the SPCA, he may help little old ladies cross the road. Yet, by the very nature of the capitalist system, he *must* treat his workers as "equipment" rather than as "people", if his business is to survive. He has absolutely no alternative but to treat his workers in the same manner as his most ruthless heartless uncaring competitor, since if he does not – if he voluntarily raises his labor costs above those of his competitors – he'd be bankrupt and out of business in a short time.

It is not the people who make up the capitalist system that are the problem – it is the social system itself, which forces *everyone* to act in a selfish and greedy manner, whether they want to or not. Capitalism, as a social/economic system, inexorably forces everyone down to the lowest possible moral level, as each owner either seeks to gain an advantage over the others, or loses out to those who do.

The workers thus come to realize that fighting against their individual factory owners, or even replacing them with kinder, gentler people, does not provide a solution to their problems. It is the *entire social system* that produces and rewards greed, avarice, and exploitation – and therefore it is the entire social system that must be destroyed and replaced.

The gap between what the capitalists say and what they do, forces the workers to address this imbalance, and to attempt to gain some measure of control over the workplace. This process is helped by several trends which are operating in the capitalist workplace.

Early capitalist enterprises were essentially vertical organizations, which were overseen by a single owner/manager. Once the overproduction crisis forces these enterprises to expand and diversify, however, they must adopt a more horizontal method of management in order to monitor the tasks of coordinating and integrating a wide range of operations. In this method of management, pioneered by the Japanese, it is necessary to integrate the workers in the shop more fully into the management process, through the use of work teams, quality circles and autonomous project teams.

This has the effect of expanding (both legally and in practice) the gap between ownership and management. The early owner/manager was forced to make his own investment and managerial decisions, and thus could justify his appropriation of surplus value as a "reward" for making good business decisions.

In the modern corporation, however, ownership rests in the stockholders, who perform no management functions at all—they simply hire a layer of professional managers to do this for them. The stockholder-capitalist makes no decisions, performs no labor and produces no commodity. He receives his surplus value simply by virtue of the fact that he owns capital.

These trends within capitalism, then, demonstrate that the capitalist is parasitical and superfluous. Managers who perform their tasks in behalf of the stockholder-capitalists can do them just as well in behalf of the employees in the plant and the people in the surrounding community. Furthermore, the joint worker/management teams formed by the "industrial democracy" movement demonstrate that the professional managers themselves are unnecessary, and that all of their functions can be taken over by an elected council of worker representatives.

The most significant step which has been taken in this direction has been the legal addition of local community and worker representatives onto corporate boards of directors. In Germany, "co-determination" laws allow union representatives to sit on corporate decision-making boards. In the US, laws have been passed which give local communities limited voices in matters such as plant closings.

This trend towards joint worker-community decision-making marks the beginning of a new form of social structure that can do away with the capitalists and their managers. At first, the quality circles produced by the "industrial democracy" movement take the form of "advisory boards", made up of worker and management representatives.

Over time, through militant shop floor actions, the worker representatives must grow to have more power and influence over these councils, and to provide them with real decision-making power.

In the final stages of the class struggle, these quality circles can be expanded into factory councils, which network with other factory councils to produce true worker's councils. These worker's councils are quasi-governmental, and serve as a general strike committee and the focus of revolutionary power. When the bourgeois state has been broken by the general strike and militant armed actions, the worker's councils take their place, and serve as the basis for the administration of the socialist mode of production.

The worker's council is thus the proletarian government of the future in embryo. It is the political form which is taken by the socialist economic order.

The theory and practice of the worker's council government will closely parallel that of the Paris Commune and the original Russian *soviets*. All council representatives are elected by direct universal suffrage; all are elected to short terms and can be recalled at any time. Terms of office are strictly limited. Positions of authority are thus regularly rotated among the members, allowing each individual to develop a wide range of skills and decision-making abilities.

Each ward is governed by an autonomous local council, made up of elected representatives of the factory councils and communities in the area. Regional matters are handled by regional councils, and national coordination is done by the national council. In all cases, however, the autonomy of the local councils is paramount. The central bodies exist only to coordinate the actions of the local councils.

This structure is analogous to that envisioned by the syndicalists, and it is indeed the opinion of most council communists that the socio-political theories of the anarcho-syndicalists are particularly well-suited to the tasks of a self-liberated working class organization.

Marx himself, of course, was bitterly opposed to the anarcho-syndicalists, and fought bitter faction fights with the Bakuninists during his lifetime. Most of Marx's opposition to syndicalism was, however, based on a mistaken conception of the future development of capitalism.

Marx was writing at a time when the productive forces of capitalism were just beginning to develop, and no one could be sure how quickly productive ability could be expanded. He was able to see the rapid expansion of productive forces which capitalism had made available, but never saw the actual level of these forces which would later develop under monopoly capitalism.

Marx, based on his contemporary studies, expected that capitalism would never be able to fully develop these productive forces on its own. This was not because he doubted capitalism's ability to continuously expand its productive ability, but because he believed he was witnessing the contradictions and stresses that would soon tear capitalism apart. Until the end of his life, Marx expected the socialist revolution to come very soon, and thus remove capitalism before these productive forces could be fully developed.

Since, he assumed, the capitalist productive forces would not be fully developed before the socialist revolution, Marx expected that it would fall to the socialist system to complete this development. After the revolution, Marx thought, the working class would have to expand productive ability to high levels on its own. It would also have to fully integrate political and economic functions into one administrative apparatus, and develop these structures into a communist mode of production.

This economic development, if it was to be done under the guidance of the working class, had to be done through economic planning, and this necessitated a centralized state that controlled all economic resources. Thus, Marx argued for a period of "socialism" — a state dictatorship of the proletariat, to carry out this economic expansion before dying off and allowing "communism" to take over. This socialist system, Marx concluded, would have to remain until the planning apparatus could do its job and produce highly developed productive forces.

At first, Marx saw the socialist revolution as being merely the capture of the existing bourgeois central government, with the proletariat using this apparatus to nationalize the economy and plan for maximum economic production. This, Marx concluded, would be done by forcible revolution where necessary, or, in open countries like the US, Britain or France, could be done simply by using universal suffrage to capture the state through the election of a socialist party, thus legislating socialism into existence.

After the Paris Commune, however, Marx changed his mind and decided that the old bourgeois state apparatus was not suitable for the working class's purposes, and that the workers would have to introduce their own governmental structure — one which would be able to take control of the nation's economic resources and expand them to the necessary levels. This could not be done in any way other than a violent insurrection.

Marx's conflict with Bakunin centered on this "dictatorship of the proletariat". In essence, Marx wanted to use a proletarian state to develop the productive forces which would be left by capitalism until they were strong enough for the abundant super-productive economy necessary for communism. Bakunin, on the other hand, wanted to develop productive forces using independent communes, not a central planning process administered by a socialist state.

The Leninists, who took power in a country that was economically backwards and undeveloped, found the Marxian idea of the central "proletarian state" to be perfectly suited to their need for rapid industrialization. They were thus able to use Marxist phraseology to justify their centrally planned industrialization program, which developed high productive abilities in the economy, but did it in the class interests of the bureaucrats rather than the working class.

In retrospect, we can see that Marx was wrong, as modern capitalist development has made much of Marx's reasoning irrelevant. Today, capitalism itself has already developed extraordinarily high levels of productivity, has already begun integrating the corporate economy with the political state, and has already begun to face the problem of distribution of abundant commodities according to need. There is, we can now see, no need for a "transitional" socialist government to accomplish these things after the revolution.

There is thus no need anymore to postulate a "socialist" state which replaces the capitalist state with a "dictatorship of the proletariat". It is not necessary to plan for a rapid expansion of productive ability, because monopoly capitalism has already produced it, and has already brought about rapid economic development.

Indeed, the enormous productivity of the corporate economy has forced it, in its own interests, to begin the process of socializing the economy. The huge capitals of the corporations steadily destroy the smaller sectors of the economy – small businesses are now economic non-entities with little real power in the economy. They continue to exist only insofar as the corporations have not yet decided to either buy them out or drive them out of business. This has the effect of steadily uniting society's economic resources under a small number of managements. The economic power of the corporations and their control over economic processes allows them to circumvent the marketplace entirely, and to deliberately plan for both short-term and long-term economic investment and growth. The concentration of stock ownership amongst the owning class not only separates ownership from management, and produces collectivized ownership rather than individual proprietorship, but leads to the economy's management functions being placed into the hands of a professional managerial layer, which gets its authority not from the fact that it owns capital, but that it is *elected* by the social class of capital-owners.

In effect, the corporate stockholding class is building a rough framework for a socialist economy. They have already destroyed the classical capitalist economy of small individual shopkeepers, and have consolidated each industry under a single management. They have already destroyed private individual ownership of industry, and replaced it with socialized joint ownership by groups of stockholders. They have already introduced short-term and long-term planning, at the local, regional, national and international levels, to undermine competition, and thus are destroying the "marketplace" as a method of production and distribution. And they have already introduced the practice of running the economy through elected representatives who are responsible and revocable by their electors.

In short, everything the socialists want to do, the corporate class has already started. Of course, the stockholding class is very careful to monopolize all the decision-making power and economic benefits from their socialized system into their own hands, and to keep it out of everyone else's hands. Nevertheless, the corporations are themselves building the basis for socialized production and distribution. In the end, all the workers will have to do is organize ourselves to kick the corporados out of power, and then run the new socialized economy democratically, for everyone's benefit.

Thus, the tasks of a socialist revolution consist of replacing the bourgeois institutions with *social*-ist ones, with new institutions of social hegemony that can carry on communist production and distribution from the start. The social relationships which carry out these tasks must be rooted in the institutions which were used by the working class to carry out the revolution; in other words, the revolutionary bodies must be the nucleus of the communist system. These bodies are the worker's councils. In this manner, Marxism and syndicalism can be seen to be merely different ways of looking at the same problem — that of building and running a social-ist society.

Building the worker's councils is a job for labor unions, but not the reformist labor unions such as the AFL-CIO. This task must be carried out by revolutionary syndicalist unions, that have as their goal, not that of gaining better wages, but of abolishing the wage system.

The most famous proponents of this view in the US are the Industrial Workers of the World, or "Wobblies". The IWW was at the zenith of its power in the early 1910's, when the council communist movement was beginning in Europe, and Wobbly philosophy had a large impact on council theory; the Dutch council communist Anton Pannekoek found himself to be in "substantial agreement" with IWW literature he obtained.

The IWW was formed specifically as a revolutionary alternative to the AFL "business unions". While Gompers and the AFL preached "A Fair Day's Wages for a Fair Day's Work", the IWW preached "The Working Class and the Employing

Class Have Nothing in Common." The ultimate Wobbly goal is the general strike, in which workers are organized into One Big Union, collectively fold their arms and sit down to "lock out the capitalists". The IWW organizes its workers into Industrial Unions, which are set up with the intention of running the workplaces democratically after the bosses are deposed. This strategy is summed up in the IWW motto, "We are building a new world within the shell of the old."

The council communists believe that the political and social principles of syndicalism must be combined with the socio-economic analysis of Marxism to become truly proletarian in character and to be capable of guiding the working class to liberation. Marxism provides the intellectual and theoretical weapons—a conception of how capitalism works and how social change develops. Syndicalism, on the other hand, provides the material weapons for the struggle—the general strike, militant direct action, industrial organization. Thus, syndico-Marxism, rather than Marxism-Leninism, is the only authentically proletarian outlook which can produce the socialist mode of production.

The Leninist vanguard party is not well-suited to the self-liberation of the working class, and the council communist movement must reject it as a model. The most practical form of organization for the task of worker self-emancipation is that envisioned by Marx and practiced by the syndicalists—the organization of One Big Union of All the Workers.

Marx never considered that the revolutionary organization would be made up of a small group of professional revolutionary zealots. Instead, he envisioned the organization developing as a result of day to day struggles with the capitalists.

At first, Marx foresaw, the workers would be driven by the circumstances of their existence to seek higher wages and better working conditions, and would be forced to organize themselves into trade unions to fight for these things.

Eventually, the workers would be forced to fight in the political arena as well, and the need would arise for a political organization — the labor party.

These actions, however, will not by themselves be enough to break the power of the capitalists, since the trade unions and the labor party cannot function outside of the capitalist relationships which produced them. They are important, not for their immediate results, which are ephemeral at best, but in schooling the working class in methods of organization, solidarity and concerted struggle. It is not the immediate results of these fights that are important — it is the mere fact that the workers are fighting, that they are consciously seeking a predetermined goal and are becoming more proficient at fighting for it.

When circumstances at last reach the point where the working class realizes that the owners can be directly challenged, the trade union and the labor party will give way to a new form of organization — the worker's council.

The worker's councils, which grow in power in the final stages of the class struggle, are the logical successors to the trade unions and labor parties. The councils provide the working class with the organizational framework needed to organize itself as a whole, to expand its revolutionary actions and to coordinate and direct the struggle. Since the arena for the revolutionary struggle between labor and capital is in the workplace, the working class revolution must be fought in the factories and the enterprises. The worker's councils provide the framework for this struggle.

EIGHT:
Revolutionary Action

On the practical level of revolutionary action, the worker's council movement presents new strategies and options for the working class. While the Leninist parties are reduced to measuring their "revolutionary influence" by the number of party members and the circulation of their party newspaper, the council movement is concerned with direct revolutionary action and the construction of a mass movement. The worker's councils serve as the embryo of the future socialist government. They represent the institutions and relationships which are growing within the shell of capitalism. The measure of the power of the council communist movement, then, consists in the amount of power and influence the workers exert at the point of production.

Each factory council becomes in essence a tiny proletarian government, defending the interests of the workers against the capitalists and actively seeking to place more power in the hands of the working class. Thus, the task of the worker's council is to become a "dual power", a working class socio-political entity existing alongside of and in opposition to the bourgeois state. The goal of the revolutionary movement may then be summed up in the slogan, "All power to the worker's councils."

The organization of the working class, then, is inextricably linked with the development of worker's councils. This type of revolutionary "party" is not concerned with bourgeois politics or elections, nor is it involved with sterile discussions on obscure points of doctrine or party discipline. It is a fighting organization built for action—rather than arguing and planning for some future revolution, the worker's councils build the revolutionary institutions within the old order of things. In this view, the revolution is something to be *made*, not merely waited for.

The worker's council is thus irreversibly tied to direct action. The bulk of these actions—slowdowns, sabotage, work-to-rule, the general strike, etc.—can be carried out nonviolently, and can gain a measure of power for the workers. In order to seize actual control of the economy, however, the workers will have to fight, and armed defensive actions will become necessary.

Obviously, given a choice between war and peace, only a fool would willingly choose war. If it were possible to replace the capitalist mode of production with the socialist using peaceful and nonviolent means, each of us would gladly lay our weapons aside.

Such a peaceful transition is, however, improbable. The bourgeoisie has proven consistently in the past that, when its class interests are threatened, it is quite willing to resort to police and military force to attack the working class movement and defend its own position (the 1877 Upheaval, the IWW trials, the Palmer Raids, Sacco and Vanzetti, McCarthy, COINTELPRO, the Patriot Act). The capitalists will fight to maintain their position of privilege, and if we are to win, we must be willing to fight against these forces—and not only fight against them, but defeat them. If we do not defeat the forces of the capitalists in the streets and at the barricades, we will lose and our revolution will go down in defeat.

It should be obvious that the workers cannot hope to stand in face-to-face combat with the armed forces of the industrial nations and defeat them. One of the main goals of the revolutionary movement must be to organize insurrectionary circles among the "workers in uniform" — those who, out of economic hardship, have been forced into the "volunteer" armed forces. If the armed forces are unreliable, the bourgeoisie will be severely limited in its ability to repress the radical working class movement.

In the meantime, armed working class defense must take the form of hit-and-run attacks, of guerrilla warfare.

Rural guerrilla warfare, as practiced by Mao, Giap and Che, depends on the existence of the proper conditions for struggle — large expanses of inaccessible territory, low population density, and few means of transportation and communication — which allow the guerrillas to establish a floating stronghold, a *foco*. This strongpoint is used to build up an armed movement which captures the countryside, surrounds the urban areas and overwhelms them. Without these conditions, the focoists conclude, armed guerrilla struggle is impossible.

In the late 1960's, however, a new form of armed action appeared — the "urban guerrilla". The urban guerrillas rejected not only the focoist reliance on favorable geographical conditions, but also the entire Leninist viewpoint on social revolution.

One of the chief theorists of the urban guerrilla movement was Abraham Guillen, a Spanish anarcho-Marxist who had settled in Uruguay. Guillen declared that the Communist Parties had been reduced to reformist tools of the Soviet Union, and could no longer be looked to for guidance in revolutionary action. The Communist Party leaders, Guillen wrote, "have made of Marxism a parade of portraits of Marx,

Engels and Lenin; the thought behind each is interpreted after the manner of Christian doctrine by certain sects and churches. Thus the images are venerated, but not the substance":

> The Soviet bureaucracy is only nominally Marxist; its fundamental concern is industrialization on the basis of nationalization, not the socialization of wealth. Control over the economy is exercised by a centralized and totalitarian administration without worker's participation . . . with greater vigor than the bourgeoisie ever did.

> Underlying spurious proletarian internationalism is a national chauvinism which tramples on the interests of other Communist parties by sacrificing those interests to Soviet objectives.

Guillen rejected the Leninist reliance on "objective conditions", and argued that social change was produced by people, not by circumstances. While Che Guevara was an authentic revolutionary hero, Guillen pointed out, his strategy of guerrilla warfare based on rural conditions could not work in urban industrialized nations. "If 70% of a country's population is urban," he pointed out, "the demography and the economy must dictate the specific rules of the strategy of revolutionary combat":

> Between a favorable territory and a favorable population. the army of liberation must choose the population and not the terrain. Only a guerrilla force with the support of the population is able to bring about the revolutionary war of the armed people, against which the most powerful regular army is helpless.

Guillen also pointed out that the majority of the focoist guerrillas are drawn from the radical intelligentsia and the student movement, not from the rank-and-file workers. This separates the guerrillas from the aims and desires of the workers, and leads the fighters into fatal strategic errors. Guillen writes, "The struggle is limited mainly to engagements between the guerrillas on one side and the army and police on the other. In these encounters, the people are caught in the middle, leaving a political vacuum which only a different kind of guerrilla movement can fill; one providing support for all popular acts of protests, strikes, demonstrations, student rebellions, etc."

"Youthful Leninists," Guillen says, "without working class experience, without having suffered directly from the effects of capitalist exploitation, aspire to liberate the workers without the workers' own revolutionary intervention." Such a movement cannot succeed, he concluded, because it lacked the one essential ingredient for the success of any guerrilla force — popular support. "If the bulk of the population does not support an action for liberation . . . then every tactical victory leads to an ultimate strategic defeat."

If urban guerrillas cannot continually disappear among the population of a great city, then they lack the political prerequisites for making a revolution.

If urban guerrillas are to be successful, says Guillen, they must center their actions around the militant labor movement, and must devote their resources to "directing trade union struggles or introducing workers' self-management":

> Once revolutionaries are in command of their own house, then they are ready for revolutionary action in depth; the occupation of factories that operate at less than full capacity, the transformation of these into producers' cooperatives or self-managed enterprises, and preparation for the seizure of political power.

> To make a social revolution it is necessary to overthrow by violence the old ruling class, to dissolve the old social relations between exploited and exploiting classes, to create a new mode of production (socialism in place of capitalism), to organize new juridical relations and to form a direct government of the people, with organs of production.

In other words, Guillen concluded, the aim of the militant guerrilla movement must be to support and protect the worker's councils.

Throughout the 1960's, a number of guerrilla groups experimented with such tactics. In 1971, the Uruguayan Revolutionary Popular Organization (OPR-33) used armed action to support a strike at the Portland Cement Company in Montevideo. Within a year of this action, OPR-33 settled a textile strike by kidnapping the owner's son, and won recognition for the union and payment of wages lost during the strike. During this same time, the Argentinean Peoples' Revolutionary Army (ERP) kidnapped the general managers of the Swift plant in Rosario and the Fiat plant in Buenos Aires in support of strikes there. The Swift manager was exchanged for the rehiring of all suspended workers, a reduction of production quotas and the distribution of $60,000 in food, clothing and schoolbooks to the poor working class neighborhoods. Tupamaros guerrillas from Uruguay often hijacked food trucks and left them parked, unlocked, in the poorer sections of Montevideo.

Guillen thus discarded the Leninist strategy of using the vanguard *foco* to take over the state and bring the Leninist party to power, and instead argued in favor of direct mass action to bring about "the self-management of production by the workers themselves; a libertarian socialism without a bureaucracy as the new ruling class."

Guillen referred to his councilist outlook as "anarcho-Marxism", as a "reconciliation of Marx with Bakunin":

> Anarcho-Marxism is the revolutionary science of our epoch; Marxist in its economic conceptions of capitalism and the means of overcoming them; anarchist in its conception of direct democracy, self-managed enterprises and federations of freely associated workers. Marxist and anarchist forms of socialism are reconciled in the socialism of self-management, when the organs of production and administration are based on direct democracy and not on the bureaucratic state disguised as an illusory "dictatorship of the proletariat".

One of the most instructive uses of armed force came in Italy in the 1970's. In 1968 and 1969, a wave of strikes rolled across Italy. As these strikes became more violent and more militant, workers in the Pirelli tire plant in Milan and the Monfalcone shipyard in Venice gave up on their conservative trade union bureaucracies and set up their own United Rank-

and-File Committees (CUB) to direct their own militant labor actions. These councils were composed of elected worker representatives and people from the surrounding community (usually radical student leaders). By 1969, over 100 large factories in Italy had established CUBs.

The labor rebellion reached its peak in 1969, known as "Hot Autumn". All over Italy, CUBs directed militant (and often violent) strikes and factory occupations. On several occasions, the town halls were also occupied by labor insurgents. By 1970, the CUBs in Milan met and formed the Metropolitan Political Collective (CPM) to coordinate their actions. In addition to supporting strikes and labor revolts, the CPM expanded its activities to include seizing and occupying vacant buildings and turning them over to poor working class families.

In 1970, the urban guerrilla group Red Brigades was formed to provide armed support for CPM's actions. The original Red Brigade unit was formed in the giant Mirafiori Fiat works in Turin, but within a year, the Brigades had strongholds in Fiat, Alfa-Romero and Simiens plants all over northern Italy.

The Red Brigades rejected the "leadership" of the Italian Communist Party, arguing that, in addition to being a tool of Moscow with no real connection to the Italian workers, the Party simply was not suited for the tasks of building a democratic rank-and-file movement. "It is not the 'betrayal' of the leadership," the Brigades concluded, "as much as the structural inadequacy of the weapon they use, that is, their organization, which is at the root of it all."

The Brigades were formed specifically to defend the militant rank-and-file CUBs. "Our point of view," the guerrillas announced, "is that the armed struggle in Italy must be conducted by an organization that is the direct expression of the class movement. Because of this we are working toward the organization of factory and neighborhood worker cells in the industrial and metropolitan centers, where revolt and exploitation are primarily concentrated." The Brigades supported the militant workers by burning the cars of managers and by adopting a tactic known as "knee-capping", in which unpopular managers and foremen were shot through the legs.

At the height of their power, the Red Brigades had over a thousand active members and hundreds of thousands of sympathizers. After a period of several years, however, the Brigades fell under the control of radical students, who steered the group away from direct labor support and towards more overtly political action. Red Brigade guerrillas began to kidnap and knee-cap prominent Italian political officials, culminating in the kidnapping and execution of former Christian Democrat Premiere Aldo Moro. As the organization moved away from militant labor support, the guerrillas lost the support of the radical rank-and-file, and were the easy victims of police infiltration and repression. By the 1980's, the Red Brigades no longer existed.

The Brigades had unfortunately failed to heed their own advice:

> No armed revolutionary movement which struggles for power can measure up to the struggle without being able to realize two fundamental conditions; (1) measure itself against power at all levels . . . and naturally demonstrate the ability to know how to survive these levels of conflict, and (2) bring forth an alternative power in the factories and workers' neighborhoods.

The Brigades were able to exist for a period of several years, and thus fulfilled the first of their two conditions; by abandoning the CUB councils, however, they lost their support and thus their ability to survive police repression.

Thus, we can see that the proletarian revolution cannot succeed unless it has both a mass base and the physical means of struggle which will allow it to win. The council movement's attitudes towards the other groups of the Left must therefore be based on two questions—that of party democracy and that of direct action and armed struggle.

A party that does not demonstrate party democracy and direct ties to the working class movement as a whole is not a proletarian party at all—it is merely an elitist clique which attempts to set itself above the workers. Council communists can have no interest in such an organization.

On the other hand, an organization which does not favor armed struggle and direct action is not serious about destroying the power of the bourgeoisie, and is indistinguishable in practice from any other liberal reform group. The serious revolutionary movement is interested in overthrowing the capitalists and in seizing the means of production, and this can be done only through armed action.

At the same time, the council movement must reject the strategy of those who attempt to use armed struggle for its own sake. Armed groups such as the United Freedom Front, the Weathermen, the Red Army Fraction and the Japanese Red Army all attempt to "raise consciousness" by carrying out symbolic armed attacks on capitalist economic and political power structures. Their rationale—that the masses are ignorant and must be prodded into action by the example of the revolutionary elite—is the same as that of the Leninists. The council movement must reject this notion of "propaganda of the deed", and condemn any armed struggle that does not have as its goal that of forming and expanding a revolutionary working class movement organized into worker's councils. Picking up guns and taking to the streets is the *last* thing a revolutionary organization does, not the first.

The sole purpose of armed struggle must be that of strengthening and protecting the worker's councils, allowing them to grow into a power independent of the capitalist structures which they will replace. In our current stage of struggle, no authentic working class organization exists which is strong enough to coordinate an armed struggle for power. The current task of the revolutionary movement, therefore, is to build up a foundation of syndicalist worker's councils to fight for democracy in the workplace and for a larger role for workers in the management of the enterprises and factories.

This process must be supported with legal steps and with extralegal support in the form of strikes, sabotage, and direct actions.

Currently, there is little role to be fulfilled by armed guerrilla actions. As the worker's councils mature and produce a revolutionary situation, however, the need for armed action grows.

In the beginning of the struggle, when the working class forces are weak and scattered, the task of armed action is simply to defend the worker's councils from the repressive forces of the capitalist state. Armed force is purely defensive, and takes the form of resistance to police raids and other repressive actions.

As the movement grows, the need to defend the councils from armed repression grows with it. At a certain point, moreover, the working class movement will be capable of carrying out limited actions to combat and weaken the bourgeois power structure. Armed actions have the political goal of demonstrating that the capitalists are not invincible and that they can be defeated by the working class's attacks.

As the class struggle breaks into open warfare, the councils serve as provisional government bodies, defended by the armed strength of the working class. When it becomes possible to contest power in the streets, to bring to a head the "dual power" contradiction, the councils serve to coordinate the general strike and the armed uprising which sweeps away the capitalist power structure and places control of the economy in the hands of the working class organizations.

This process was approximately followed by the *soviets* in Russia, which took on the form of a council government of local producers. The *soviets*, however, neglected (with the notable exception of Makhno) to build an armed wing to defend themselves, and thus were unable to offer any resistance when the Bolsheviks took over the *soviet* apparatus and distorted it for their own ends.

If the socialist movement is to bring the anti-capitalist revolution to its conclusion, then, it must be organized along the proper framework. The structure of this framework is determined by the need to survive the repressive efforts of the bourgeoisie and by the necessity that the revolutionary organs serve as the nucleus for the future socialist system. Therefore, the worker's council apparatus must be decentralized and based on widespread working class support and participation.

Each local worker's council must take on the combined duties of a local government, a factory manager, a strike committee, and a garrison commander. Under the fairly open conditions of the capitalist republic, it will be possible for the councils to carry on much of their work openly and legally. However, the councils are almost certain to be suppressed once they begin to pose a serious challenge to power, and must make provisions to carry on their work illegally, "underground". The armed wing of the worker's councils must always exist underground.

The task of defending the council and its actions from the suppression of the bourgeoisie falls to the armed wing of the movement, which serves as a sort of local militia for the working class. The strategies of the urban guerrilla force were set out by Carlos Marighella, who fought with several urban guerrilla groups in Brazil during the 1960's. Marighella laid out his tactics in *The Minimanual of the Urban Guerrilla*.

Since, in the beginning of the struggle, the armed forces of the working class are too weak to stand in toe-to-toe combat with the professional armed forces of the capitalist state, the armed wing must adopt the tactics of the urban resistance network. "The principle task of the urban guerrilla," says Marighella, "is to distract, to wear out, to demoralize the militarists, the military dictatorship and its repressive forces." As the armed wing of the worker's councils, the guerrillas provide armed support for the activities of the council, and liberate the supplies and materials needed by the revolutionary forces. In all these instances, the military struggle is subordinate to, but complementary with, the struggle to win control in the workplace.

Since the military wing of the revolutionary forces will experience repression most directly, it must be effectively organized if it is to survive and carry out its tasks. "In order to function," Marighella pointed out, "the urban guerrillas must be organized into small groups." Most urban guerrilla forces are divided into five-person teams, made up of members who have known each other for a long time. Each team is free to operate independently within the general strategic framework adopted by the worker's councils. "Within it," writes Marighella, "guerrilla operations and tactics are planned, launched and carried through to success."

Although the actions of the guerrillas must be coordinated by the councils, the freedom of action of the guerrilla teams must be respected. This decentralized structure allows the guerrillas to act on their own, without waiting for "orders from above". This gives them the ability to act quickly in response to changing circumstances and chance opportunities. "This method of action," Marighella points out, "eliminates the need for knowing who is carrying out which actions, since there is free initiative and the only important point is to increase substantially the volume of urban guerrilla activity, in order to wear out the government and force it onto the defensive."

This compartmentalized independence also makes it extremely difficult for the repressive forces of the capitalist state to infiltrate the guerrilla forces. Since each member of the guerrilla team knows the others, it is nearly impossible for the police to insert a spy or informer into their ranks.

The organization of the worker's councils and their armed wing must be loose and decentralized, to allow the work to continue even in the face of armed repression. Marighella writes that guerrillas should use autonomous local units, "each self-contained and operating separately, to disperse the government forces in their pursuit of a thoroughly fragmented organization, instead of offering the dictatorship the opportunity to concentrate its forces of repression on the destruction of one tightly-organized system operating throughout the country." Abraham Guillen echoes, "Excessive centralization of authority makes an organization rigid and vulnerable; once the repressive forces discover a single thread, they can begin looking for the spool."

Because the local units are complete in and of themselves, the forces of repression can only stamp out the revolutionary movement by infiltrating and killing each local unit. In the face of popular support for the revolutionaries, this will prove to be an impossible task.

In addition, Marighella concludes, the decentralized guerrilla network is the best means to prevent the militant working class organizations from degenerating into a centralized bureaucracy. "The old-type hierarchy," he says, "the style of the traditional Left, doesn't exist in our organization."

The structure of the militant working class organization evolves slowly during the struggle, from the bottom upwards. Initially, the council movement consists of scattered factory councils which agitate for reforms and economic democracy within the workplace. These may even begin within the existing trade union apparatus.

As the class struggle deepens, however, more and more of these factory councils are set up, and they turn more directly to the question of workplace control. As they become more militant and openly hostile to the bosses, local worker's councils are set up to coordinate the actions of various factory councils. This step marks the pinnacle of the class struggle — the councils will now actively defend themselves and their position as a "dual power".

The militant labor struggles of the worker's councils must be supported by the armed actions of the urban guerrillas. A major task of the guerrillas, Marighella noted, was "the occupation of factories and schools during strikes":

> The strike is a model of action employed by the urban guerrillas in work centers and schools to damage the enemy by stopping work and study activities. Because it is one of the weapons most feared by the exploiters and oppressors, the enemy uses tremendous fighting power and incredible violence against it. The strikers are taken to prison, suffer beatings, and many of them are assassinated.

One of the primary tasks of the guerrilla fighters will be to defend those who carry out such actions from the police and the armed forces.

The worker's councils will also move to expand their power along international lines. As we have seen, the interests of the workers and the neo-colonies must be supported through an international labor movement. The exploitation of the neo-colonies is a vital necessity for the monopolists if they are to escape the effects of the overproduction crisis. A necessary part of socialist strategy, then, must consist of denying this outlet to the monopolists, of cutting off the flow of wealth from the neo-colonies.

The more numerous are the anti-imperialist revolutions in the neo-colonies, the more quickly the flow of wealth declines and the more profoundly monopolist capitalism is thrown into crisis. For this reason, socialists in the monopolist countries must wholeheartedly support national liberation struggles in the neo-colonies. Each victory in this struggle hastens the collapse of international monopolism.

This does not mean, however, that these national liberation movements will, after gaining power, be capable of instituting a socialist mode of production. A socialist structure is above all dependent upon the existence of a highly developed industrial infrastructure which has produced a high level of productivity and material abundance. The neo-colonies, whose economic development has been deliberately stunted by the monopolist nations, lack the resources for this.

Thus, while revolutionary movements in the neo-colonies are indispensable for bringing about the conditions for the introduction of socialism, they cannot carry out this process by themselves. It is up to the working class of the monopolist nations to do this, to seize the productive forces built up by capitalism and make socialist economic relationships possible.

The task of the council movement are then clear. We must begin to build a network of worker's councils which can begin to take control of the workplace and serve as the nucleus for the socialist movement. We must begin to lay plans for an armed resistance movement which can protect and defend these councils. Finally, we must work to expand the international struggle, to tie militant workers all over the globe into a single worldwide revolutionary network.

This, it is obvious, will be a long and protracted process. At the present stage of struggle, the labor movement is still enthralled with the idea of reformism, and has not moved beyond a narrow national framework.

Many of the larger capitalist enterprises, however, are being forced to introduce the idea of worker's committees and quality circles which "advise" management on a limited number of decisions. This capitalist program of "industrial democracy" can serve as the starting point for the development of a truly revolutionary network. The size and scope of these committees must be expanded greatly through militant actions. The labor movement must fight for a larger role in management and decision-making, until the worker committees have an active and important role in every management function.

At this point, these committees must be transformed into authentic worker's councils, made up of elected and rotated representatives of the workers. These worker's councils must fight to become the de facto management of the enterprise, capable of dispensing with the owners and the professional managers and running the plant by itself.

Successful socialist revolution therefore depends on two factors — the existence of revolutionary conditions and the existence of a working class organization which is prepared to seize the moment and act in those conditions. We can do little to hasten the time when these conditions will re-appear, but we can do everything to build up the organization that these conditions will require. We must prepare a developed international network of worker's councils and an armed movement which is capable of defending this network. These are the tasks of the socialist movement.

CONCLUSION

The revolutionary working class movement, it appears, stands on the threshold of a new level of struggle. The national struggle of the working class against its own bourgeoisie has expanded to its limits, and the expansion of this struggle to an international level is now a necessary task. At the same time, reformist trade union activity is fast approaching its limits. Now, instead of merely altering the worker-owner relationship to make it more comfortable for the working class, the movement must set its sights on smashing this relationship, of abolishing the wage system and dismantling bourgeois social structures.

The present working class organizations are not suited to these tasks. Within trade union or "Communist Party" parameters, the working class will never be able to overcome capitalist hegemony and seize control. This is not merely because the leaders of these organizations are corrupt or dishonest or because they have accommodated themselves to the capitalist system—although all of these dangers are present and must be combated. Rather, the weakness of the working class movement lies in the fact that its organizational structures are incapable of carrying out the tasks which face it.

If the working class is to organize along international lines, if it is to defend itself from repression, if it is to seize control of the workplace, it must move beyond the stage of trade unions and centralized political factions. It must become a force of itself and for itself.

Only one form of organization is suited to these tasks — the worker's councils. Only the working class organized as a whole into One Big Union will be able to carry out the tasks which have set themselves before us. Only then can we truly build the new world within the shell of the old.

www.ingramcontent.com/pod-product-compliance
Lightning Source LLC
Chambersburg PA
CBHW060907280326
41934CB00007B/1218